Do, Review, Learn, Apply:

A simple guide to experiential learning

Bill Dennison
Roger Kirk

Blackwell Education

© Bill Dennison, Roger Kirk 1990

First published 1990
Published by Basil Blackwell Limited
108 Cowley Road
Oxford OX4 1JF
England

British Library Cataloguing in Publication Data
Dennison, W. F. (William F.)
    Do, review, learn, apply : a simple guide to experiental learning.
    1. Teaching methods : Experiential learning
    I. Title II. Kirk, Roger
    371.3

    ISBN 0–631–16838–9

Phototypeset in 11pt Plantin
by Opus, Oxford
Printed in Great Britain
by Dotesios Printers Ltd, Trowbridge, Wilts.

Contents

Acknowledgements

Our particular thanks are due to Tony Brennan and Chris Parkin, not only because of the exercises they have allowed us to use, but because of their constant encouragement, support and regular (but always constructive) criticism. It was Tony who devised and trialled *The Siding, Darlington Station, Indivisible Load, Push-Pull* and *Sum* (and produced the solutions), while Chris (with colleagues) constructed and wrote the Appraisal activity – *'I'll Help You Improve Your Driving'*.

We are also grateful to David Richards and Glyn Jones of Brathay Hall, and their ex-colleague Roger Putnam, for their support in the design and writing of Chapter 9 and the associated exercises – *Great Eggspectations* and *Centipede*.

Christian Aid were generous in their permission, allowing us to use *The Trading Game* as an example in Chapter 8.

We are also grateful to Hodder and Stoughton for permission to use the diagrams on *Water Bomb* construction (Exercises 1, 2 and 3, and Chapter 7) which were taken from *Origami* by Robert Hardin.

We also would not wish to forget the many students and fellow tutors who have tried out the exercises and whose comments (and criticisms) have helped in their re-design. It is they who determine the value of any learning activity.

Introduction

This book has four main purposes. First, and probably most practically, it adds to the stock of exercises. However, to aid the other purposes the context in which each of these new exercises was developed is considered. Second, for tutors of all levels of experience, it sets out to consider some of the benefits and problems associated with adapting the 'Do – Review – Learn – Apply' model. Third, it looks in particular at issues associated with selecting, writing and modifying materials; in parallel to this, it discusses the many day-to-day problems which must accompany experiential learning and suggests some solutions which have worked in the past. Fourth, it introduces some of the theoretical perspectives about experiential learning. A further dimension is added by outlining how the techniques of experiental learning have been extended to outdoor activities.

In Part 1 there are four chapters which discuss and analyse some of the theoretical and fundamental issues associated with experiential learning. The links between this and more transmissive styles of teaching and learning are discussed. Tutor and institutional attitudes towards experiential learning are assessed. The idea of the learning community, with the tutor as a fellow-learner, is debated. The notion of the learning cycle is explored, and the ways in which learners behave, relative to their needs and motivations, are reviewed. This section of the book finishes with a study of the limits of experiential learning, and the importance of promoting it through good example.

In Part 2, the practical issues involved in the planning of an experiential programme are considered in some detail. A number of potential problems that arise in practice are identified and methods used – if not to overcome, then certainly to ameliorate, them – are outlined. Chapters 6, 7 and 8 look at the selection, use and production of materials. In Chapter 7, the writing of a new exercise (which developed into three separate activities) is analysed from the time when the tutor perceived a need for some new material. An attempt has been made to provide a complete record of its inception, development and trialling. By contrast, Chapter 8 considers the advantages and disadvantages of using a 'ready made' exercise. Chapter 9 develops the outdoor element, while Chapter 10 looks at triumphs and disasters and suggests means of encouraging the former and avoiding the latter. This part of the book concludes by considering the vexed issue, so often raised by critics of experiential learning, that the experiences it offers are not real. Perhaps the best way to portray that reality is through the areas of proven worth where experiential learning has established itself in recent years, and these are discussed. Part 3 introduces 15 exercises previously unpublished in their original form.

During the long gestation period of Roger Kirk's earlier *Learning in Action* (Blackwell, 1987), and particularly when the 30 or so activities it described were being trialled and re-written, we became increasingly aware of the many teachers and lecturers who were using the experiential learning methods described. Often, however, they found themselves short of appropriate material. We also became aware of an even larger group of staff who were anxious to extend their range of teaching styles to include the *Do – Review – Learn – Apply* pattern of experiential work which the book tried to encourage. Less obviously, but nevertheless in evidence, were staff who had been pushed (often by falling rolls) into areas of the curriculum where they thought they ought to be using experiential learning methods.

Perhaps staff in all three groups had tried some form of experiential learning with their classes and it had proved unsuccessful. Sometimes, it seemed to us, these tutors were unsure about what would be involved if they pursued an experiential approach. Often they thought it was nothing more than 'learning by doing' – an activity with which their students had always been involved and in which they had no part. They did not appreciate, because no-one had explained to them, the subtle but highly significant difference between learning *by* doing and learning *through* doing (FEU, 1977). More than anything, though, they appeared to be discouraged by the lack of materials and ideas which they thought suitable for use with their classes.

What was most encouraging about the reaction from teachers and lecturers to *Learning in Action* was the positive opinions from staff who either had never tried experiential learning or had previously used such an approach but abandoned it. They reported that they were able to take many of the exercises to complement their existing teaching approaches. They found they could help students construct learning cycles, while learning much for (and about) themselves. The collection of exercises gave them confidence to introduce new approaches.

As was to be expected, problems were mentioned. Some exercises did not 'work' with certain groups, although all have been used successfully. Also it appears that most exercises have proved capable of use in ways the original designers had not conceived, either through tutor or student modification. In our view this is excellent, because it establishes the potential flexibility of the exercises and demonstrates adaptability in groups. An element of unpredictability can, however, create difficulties particularly for a tutor struggling for confidence, and attention is required to anticipate the unpredictable and to react to it.

The book demonstrates three fundamentals. First, experiential learning can be both successful and useful in certain areas of school and college work. Second, it is not an alternative to more traditional didactic styles of teaching and learning. Each has its place; the skill of the tutor is to decide which is the more suitable and use either didactic or experiential techniques appropriately. Third, the number of tutors confident to use either approach is growing. It is to meet their needs, and maintain this expansion, that this book has been written.

PART 1

Background

1 Learning experiences

The learning cycle

Most of what we learn comes from doing. From infancy onwards we take actions and we learn. Throughout our lives, learning is taking place all the time as a result of our experiences. So many examples are available to illustrate these processes that to describe even one or two might seem banal, or trivial. Experiential learning (as it will be called throughout this book) is ubiquitous. It goes on continuously even in formal education establishments – sometimes to the consternation of teachers and lecturers.

Essentially, this book concentrates upon situations in which tutors (the word will be used in a generic sense) attempt to organise the experiential learning of their students (taking that word generically also). They might choose to do this for two reasons. First, to improve or enhance this learning in some way. Second, to increase the rate at which learning occurs. To achieve these ends a tutor makes certain (often very simple) arrangements, and provides some materials and ideas. With these aids some semblance of structure can be achieved, to improve and accelerate the learning experience.

For the purposes of this book, therefore, most experiential learning starts with tutors organising an experience for their students: the opportunity of *Doing* something. Sometimes, with more mature groups, other (external) experiences of the students are used and the tutor does not plan a common experience. In both cases, though, what students did is discussed, perhaps as part of the whole group of participants or in conversation with a tutor. Data may have been collected about the experience, or an outsider might provide observations about the ways in which the group or individuals behaved during the experience. More generally after *Doing* there follows a *Review* stage. The first two steps of a learning cycle have, therefore, been constructed.

So far tutors have some control over the cycle. They can provide a clear framework for *Doing*. They can help motivate students to take part by persuasion and explanation, and while they cannot dictate what is actually done by individual students, they can assist in structuring particular aspects of the experience. Similarly, at the *Review* stage tutors can initiate discussion, involve students reluctant to speak, offer insights about special features of the experience and give guidance to those students who appear unable (or unwilling) to review their experiences.

In the final two stages of the cycle the tutor's role is more tangential. Having experienced, and then reviewed the experience, the intention is (of course) that the students learn and are then in a position to apply what they have learned. The stages of *Learn* and *Apply* thus complete the learning cycle shown in Figure 1.1.

The several arrows emerging from the *Apply* stage are meant to imply the numerous situations in which the skills and knowledge learned might be utilised, as well as the link sought between one learning cycle and the next. However, in the two later stages the tutor's role is changed dramatically. No matter how well organised the experience and the *Review* steps, the processes of learning and application are internal to the individual student, and well beyond the control of a tutor. While a group experience and *Review* have been offered, every student will take individual and, probably, idiosyncratic perceptions from these experiences. There are no certainties during these stages.

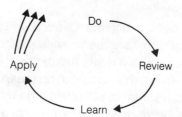

Figure 1.1 Learning cycle devised by the Development Training Advisors Group (Kirk, 1987).

Perhaps the one thing we know with certainty about human learning is that it involves extremely complex processes, few of which we have anything approaching total understanding. We are aware that learning occurs as a result of doing mainly because we can observe changes in behaviour and attitudes, and identify greater knowledge (in ourselves and others) following experience. However, even the most gifted tutor can only claim limited credit for what students learn, or how much or how quickly. The main task of a tutor is to guide each student around an individual cycle. When deliberate efforts are made by tutors to construct such cycles – in the classroom or outside – this will be termed experiential learning.

Conventional teaching

Over the years, learning by doing, as already defined, has attracted other names besides experiential learning. 'Active learning' and 'action learning' are often used, for obvious reasons. Similarly, descriptions like 'humanistic' education or 'holistic' education are not unknown, because of the focus on the individual learner rather than the material to be learned, and the thrust towards the 'wholeness' of the learning experience.

Many other learning cycles have been proposed. Their relationships to that suggested here will be discussed in the next chapter. All, however, involve the organisation of a learning experience as the key element in a learning cycle. As such the real contrast is not between one cycle and another; the significant difference lies between the strategy of experiential learning and the more conventional arrangements for teaching and learning. For it is these arrangements which tend to dominate most school and college courses.

Although the casual visitor to a school or college would be able to pick out many teaching styles – groupwork, tutor's talking, discussions, practical activities and so on – there can be no doubt that for most of the time the prevailing orthodoxy is didacticism. The tutor possesses certain knowledge or particular skills and the main business tends to concentrate upon the transmission of these to students. It is not suggested that all these activities should be replaced by tutors organising experiential learning. Both forms of learning have their place. This book tries to consider the advantages of managing experiential learning in schools and colleges and some of the practical difficulties involved.

If it is assumed that the teacher teaches and the student learns, a highly instrumental view of education follows. In this the focus quite understandably falls upon the material to be transmitted or the skills to be acquired, and all the arrangements necessary to support the processes of transfer. As a result the needs of the individual student as learner receive much less attention. At worst a pedagogy emerges which tries to provide answers when the potential learners have not yet asked the questions.

There are several reasons which account for the predominance of didacticism. It can be made to fit appropriately into the institutional framework of most schools and colleges. They must be seen to be accountable for what they try to teach their students. It is easier to designate objectives, design teaching programmes and examine students when the knowledge to be transmitted is known than it is to discuss learning cycles over which the tutor has only limited control. Most significantly, learning cycles involve individuals while the tutor has responsibility for many students and the institution for every student.

From an institutional perspective a transmissive mode appeals because of its potential for control and accountability and its economy in the use of time. A syllabus can be produced and progress through it checked. It is also attractive on account of the comparative ease with which a traditional timetable and room arrangements can be accommodated. Indeed, the latter have been constructed on the assumption that this mode will prevail. Similar thinking relates to examination procedures. Examining which knowledge and skills have been successfully transferred to groups of students is much easier than making judgements about the learning cycles of every individual student.

Tutor attitudes

The attitudes of tutors towards didacticism should not be discounted lightly. The tradition in which many have been educated themselves is important. In the main they have done well from a transmissive mode. They were taught in this way for much of their time at school and college, and went on to pass conventional examinations. Such a mode must have held some attractions or they would not have become tutors. Their long formal training has made them knowledgeable, and there are a number of reasons why they should wish to transmit this knowledge in a didactic manner.

First, as likely or not, their knowledge will be subject-based. Even when working on a cross-curricular topic they rely to a large extent on subject expertise. In the main this is the basis for their authority. For them to appear uninformed or unable to predict what might, or ought to happen, next could be perceived as a dereliction of professional duties. According to this view, tutors ought to be able to deal with every conceivable situation as it arises. The students expect that, as do parents, governors, LEA officers and employers.

Second, there is a perception that authority is related to prestige. According to this view, when a didactic approach prevails a tutor has status well above that of the students. If that approach is eschewed it follows that an authority vacuum will result. Thinking like this demonstrates a mistaken view of authority. It assumes that a tutor must *impose* authority, rather than enabling it to emerge through interest in the learning. Similarly, some tutors do not want to vacate their position as the centre of attraction, which happens when attention switches from the transmission of material to the experiential learning needs of each student.

Third, there are issues related to the attitudes, beliefs and feelings of the students. Once students leave primary school they are increasingly exposed to didactic teaching. Most accept this situation (if they reflect upon it) for a combination of reasons – the need to pass examinations, the nature of the material to be learned, the requirements of the timetable, rooms etc. For some, at least, it induces a spirit of security which tutors might wish to reinforce. Students can remain passive in a transmissive lesson. They do not have to participate in an active sense, and perhaps have what they do observed and described as part of some discussion. What they have or have not learned from the lesson will be determined some time afterwards in a test or examination.

Assumptions about the passiveness of student learning also fuel the fourth attraction of didacticism – tutor security. The combination of knowledge, status and the security needs of students make tutors feel in charge, in that they appear to control events in the classroom. Often this is true. Students behave as intended. The material of the lesson is transmitted. It is expected that the students will leave with good notes, and will be satisfied and secure because these ought to help them complete the course and pass the examination. Simultaneously, the tutor is also secure because he or she has organised activities as planned. Of course this does not always occur but when it does not, the students can be blamed for being inattentive or unruly or badly motivated towards the material; the emphasis is not on them as potential learners, but on the material to be transferred.

Shared experiences

A final attraction of more transmissive modes of teaching is that, by comparison, experiential learning is bound to seem a messy business. Many tutors, and also headteachers and college principals, find this disturbing. Organising a lesson where the main purpose is to convey certain knowledge; or arranging a laboratory class, where students are supposed to learn a particular technique or skill, present few problems. In these situations the starting point is imposed, the means easily defined and reasonably predictable, while the end point (completion of that part of the syllabus) is clear. Sometimes, but not always, overall objectives can be sub-divided into sub-objectives for each session and student progress assessed. While there will be some individualism in this assessment, and in the way the lecturer works with the class, the essential thrust is group-based. The intention is for all students to cover the same material at roughly the same pace; if this is not achieved, there are organisational difficulties.

Organising experiential learning offers new, and greater, challenges. At the nub is student-centredness and the notion of the individual student as a potential learner. Whatever learning is planned, each student comes with a background of previous experience. All have, at the start of a session, a range of needs and requirements. An important task of the tutor is to ensure that students think these may be satisfied.

Irrespective of the success of this process all have expectations (some of which may be negative) of what they might obtain from a session. Each participant has certain characteristics, affected by intellectual capacity and personality traits, which will influence the contribution made and the traditional learning situation; the difference being that in experiential learning they are part of the components with which the tutor begins to develop objectives, working patterns and possible outcomes.

The numerous differences within any group of students both emphasise the possible benefits of experiential learning and highlight the attributes required of tutors. Traditional teaching is most successful when students in a group are of about the same ability, have similar motivational and commitment patterns, start from equivalent knowledge or skill bases, and intend to reach the same end point. The less such characteristics pertain, the more the possible advantages of experiential learning. If properly organised, differences contribute to the learning experience.

All students can be offered a similar experience – for example, one which focuses on conveying information within groups. Yet this experience can only add a fraction to the previous experiences which each student brings to bear on this planned learning situation. However, many further learning opportunities are opened up through discussing and analysing the experience organised by the tutor; comparing it with previous experiences and the experiences of other group members, and so on. In this particular context (conveying information) the group could be invited to solve a problem, with each member possessing different information about it. Almost certainly, each student will have a different learning cycle as a result of this shared experience. In the first place, they hold different pieces of information; further, commitment, ability and previous experiences will all influence what each student gains from this shared experience.

With a shared group experience, such as that described above, several different elements can be engineered. One student can chair any discussion, others can negotiate specific roles, while some may watch and perform observational tasks. The tutor must accept a substantial organisational responsibility (perhaps by ensuring that all necessary duties are performed by the students themselves) and cannot abrogate responsibility for clarifying objectives, designing procedures, assessing what has been achieved and encouraging student involvement.

Sometimes a student will not wish to participate in a shared experience. Perhaps he or she sees little relevance in what is proposed, has a different priority of needs to other group members, or is embarrassed. A skilled and sensitive tutor can often take such perceptions and integrate them with the experiences of all group members – making this a learning opportunity for both the individual and the group.

The learning community

The main job of the tutor is to help organise the learning. This is quite different from teaching. Tutors cannot *make* students learn, whether through arranging a learning cycle or using a more traditional teaching style. All that can be attempted in experiential learning is to provide an opportunity, and circumstances, which are congruent with student requirements. The tutor organises and by explanation, example or persuasion, motivates the student towards a learning cycle. Sometimes this motivation is unnecessary. On other occasions it will be unsuccessful.

In practice, the range of responses to a formalised experiential learning situation will range from keen acceptance to grudging inclusion. Such attitudes, and any variations in them that accrue over time, can be used to illuminate and elucidate learning about the common experience. The tutor provides a framework by assisting students to extend their experiences, drawing out perceptions about these experiences, and introducing (where appropriate) theoretical perspectives about the learning, the experience or the topic. Although it may sound too grand, what tutors are trying to attain with their students is some form of learning community.

At first there appears to be a paradox between promoting a learning community through experiential learning and the avowed student-centredness of experiential learning. However, concentration on the needs of individual students does not preclude the possibility that they have much to learn from one another during the analysis, discussion and observation which are essential aspects of shared learning experiences. Indeed, when effectively organised, these activities provide the biggest spur to learning, especially for those students (probably the majority) who listen more attentively to their peers than to their tutors. In fact, the real paradox occurs in transmissive modes of teaching. A main advantage (when transmissive teaching is successful) is its efficiency, which is best achieved through a class working with one tutor at the same pace through identical material. Yet within this type of management students work alone. Any gains from co-operative working occur by chance. Indeed, individual students are often competing against one another in striving to achieve standards set by external examining boards.

The learning community concept is not complete, however, unless the tutor belongs to the community. For many tutors the idea that experiential learning can offer as much to them as to their students requires further explanation. Experiential learning affects both parties. The needs of tutors, as well as their previous experiences, attitudes and knowledge are very different from those of their students, but they stand to gain their own rewards as they construct their own learning cycles through assisting students learn.

Undoubtedly tutors have quite different roles from students. They are responsible for the programme. They can be held accountable if student learning does not occur. They have experience of managing and promoting learning. They are (usually) more familiar with the material used or item discussed, and certainly possess greater access to contacts, personnel, ideas and work schemes. Above all, the expectations of tutors are different. Their expectations relate to other groups of students, alternative working situations and ideas about how student learning in one set of circumstances can be adjusted or accelerated elsewhere by changes in their own behaviours or practices.

However, as for their students, factors such as self-esteem, confidence, motivation and commitment influence the learning of tutors. Group support, either from colleagues or the institution, is a significant factor. A tutor working in a conducive atmosphere, in which there is opportunity to discuss and think through experiences with colleagues, and with access to materials needed to support student work, is already part of a staff learning community. It is far more likely that such a tutor can convert this membership into a learning community involving students than it would be for a colleague denied these facilities.

If such staff find themselves working excessive hours, or taking large groups, or confronted by students with little commitment to learn, then the main objective of the tutor becomes survival, not learning. In more helpful circumstances, though, tutors' appreciation of their role as learners and members of a learning community is a major potential contributor to the effectiveness of experiential learning situations.

Structure and objectives

It is not difficult for critics of experiential learning to describe a learning community as an easy or complacent set-up. After all, tutors must regard themselves as members in order that they too may learn, so how, in such circumstances can students learn if the tutors do not know everything? Aren't they supposed to lead the students in their learning and shouldn't good leadership be based upon knowledge and awareness, providing characteristics such as the capacity to identify objectives and organise resources so that they are achieved?

In fact what is being portrayed by such criticisms is an experiential learning lacking in objectives and structure; in other words much activity but little effort to help students construct learning cycles. Experiential learning can be like this, a great deal of doing with minimal opportunity for the *Review* stage. Any learning and application which do follow (from the learning cycle) occur more by chance and coincidence than through good organisation. Although this may describe a great deal of the learning which occurs outside the school or college, it is not the type of experiential learning discussed in this book.

Experiential learning, if it is to be effective, must be both well organised and purposeful. Because the intention is to assist students construct their own learning cycle, which only they can control, it does not follow that sessions should be devoid of structure. Quite the contrary; a tutor provides a structure (through organisation, supplying materials, timing etc) within which each learning cycle can be built. Sometimes this structure may be very tight, with the tutor well aware of the next stages during a session; on other occasions some aspects of the structure may be allowed to evolve, dependent upon student response or interest. In the same way the level of direction given by a tutor (whether to the full group or part of it) can vary from low to high as demanded by the circumstances, although a highly structured and highly directed session would be indistinguishable from a didactic lesson. These issues receive more attention in later chapters.

The capacity of tutors to define objectives is another significant feature of experiential learning; it helps provide purpose for their sessions (and assists in evaluating outcomes) and also permits students to determine whether tutor objectives may be aligned with their own. This process of realignment, and, if necessary, readjustment of both tutor and student perceptions about objectives raises issues which are considered more fully in Chapter 4.

A main objective of experiential learning is to change some aspect(s) of behaviour. When a student learns how to repair a television, the change is quite obvious: new psychomotor skills are learned, which may be used again, and the student is aware of this learning. A more complex example might be where a student learns to behave assertively. If the student acts more assertively there has clearly been some learning, but the skills, attitudes, opinions and beliefs which determine the new behaviour are not easily defined or categorised. Indeed, students may not be aware of behaving more assertively. An outsider might judge that learning has occurred – about independence, relationships in a group, ways of adjusting to new situations, or functioning within constraints – and each of these will have contributed to increase effectiveness. Such observations, however, may not convince students, who may remain unsure about their assertiveness.

This introduces a second complexity – the issue of motivation. Students will accept a tutor's objectives if these do not conflict with their own priorities. They may be persuaded to accept imposed objectives, but only if they can perceive a useful outcome (to them) from the learning. They may want to be more assertive, but not see it as a priority. Even were it a priority, they may be unconvinced that what the tutor suggests will improve their assertiveness.

At other times an intention to realise behaviour change is still less clear. Courses to increase empathy or raise economic awareness of participants are good examples. They do not appear to concentrate so directly on behaviour change. Yet that is what they are trying to achieve. If people are more empathetic or have greater awareness of the economic parameters in which they live, it is not unreasonable to assume that they will react in ways they would not have done previously. This assumption, however, poses another critical question for experiential learning. Course members may be more empathetic or aware, and they can be given tests and checklists to find this out, but is it not well-nigh impossible to discover how much the learned characteristics transfer to new situations and therefore what effect they have on subsequent behaviour? (Motivational issues are discussed further in Chapter 4.)

Educational objectives

One way in which issues related to what students have learned can be considered further is to return to objectives – what is it they intend to learn? The best known analysis of educational objectives is Blooms Taxonomy (1964) in which he suggests four domains: *psychomotor* (physical activity), *cognitive* (knowledge), *affective* (feelings) and *inter-personal* (relationships with others). From the perspective of the taxonomy a student who has learned to repair televisions has acquired a knowledge *how* ie a capacity to mend specific makes with certain faults, therefore combining elements of two (psychomotor and cognitive) of the four domains of the taxonomy. Indeed the two facets of the learning become complementary with good design. Students learn some electronic theory which they apply. Successful doing motivates them towards a greater appreciation of the cognitively-based theory.

By contrast the student who has learned to be more assertive has probably included all four domains (the first two plus affective and interpersonal) in the process. Such a person has a knowledge *how* to be more assertive (through body language, verbal interactions etc) as well as knowledge *of* the range of behaviour that may lead to certain outcomes, and knowledge *that* observed behaviour is likely to indicate nervousness, confidence etc in another person.

Bloom also suggests four levels of learning – memory, understanding, application and transfer. In Chapter 3 these are related to effective learning behaviour. The more assertive learner will have proceeded through these four levels – if he or she has achieved the objective of more assertive behaviour in domestic and professional settings which neither tutor nor tutee can either predict or foresee. Of course all classifications of learning of this type are unsatisfactory in one way or another. Any learning with a practical element means an overlap in psychomotor and cognitive objectives. Similarly, the interplay of affective and interpersonal dimensions is always present, while the exact categorisation of level of learning is invariably liable to interpretation.

What the classifications do demonstrate on this occasion, though, are the greater complexities and uncertainties of experiential learning as compared to more transmissive modes of teaching. The chief foci in the latter are cognitive and (depending upon the topic) psychometric. The student memorises, understands, applies and transfers some knowledge (and skills). Each step is testable, although there may be some criticisms and doubts about the reliability and validity of the tests. Compare this to experiential learning. Because of the role of the affective and interpersonal domains a huge number of uncontrollable variables are introduced. In such circumstances, it is unwise to define objectives too precisely, but sessions will still need purpose if students are to be motivated fully.

In a traditional subject-centred course it is usually easy to frame objectives. Often this is done by an examining board. It specifies the syllabus content; sometimes it nominates the percentage of marks to be awarded for understanding, application etc. As far as the student is concerned, by organising the lessons and the material the tutor determines objectives and, external examinations notwithstanding, evaluates student performance.

This represents the conventional view of the tutor. In its own way, it is a respectable state of affairs, especially for psychomotor and cognitive domains. The design function of the tutor is well defined, as interpreter of objectives, transmitter of knowledge, and evaluator of progress; as is the role of the student as recipient. However, the arrangement only works efficiently so long as students accept this role; that is if their objectives, both for content and mode of learning, are broadly in agreement with those of the tutor.

When learning is sought which involves all four domains then the arguments against tutor domination in determining objectives become much stronger. For example, if the purpose of some sessions is to raise economic awareness among students, correct attitudes or appropriate behaviours cannot be specified. One strategy is to concentrate on cognitive items. The tutor teaches about the workings of the stock-market, or the balance of payments, perhaps. The students can be tested for memory and understanding, but not for whether their behaviour elsewhere demonstrates greater economic awareness.

As for much of experiential learning, the balance between tutor and student interests is delicate. Without a tutor it is highly improbable that a group of sixth-formers or FE students would consider economic awareness in any formal sense. The tutor specifies the overall objective, provides any materials, structures some aspects of the sessions, directs proceedings as appropriate and tries to guide each student through a learning cycle. Whether the tutor likes it or not, these are the limits of control.

Some learning, particularly in the affective and interpersonal domains, will occur despite the tutor. This is not a criticism of the tutor; it characterises a learning community. The roles of tutors and students are different, but if all members are to maximise their own learning, then the influences of everyone in deciding objectives while modifying structures and directions (originally designed by tutors) have to be accepted.

The learner not the material

Experiential learning cannot be neatly packaged. Organising it offers numerous challenges. It makes demands upon tutors over and above those associated with a more didactic approach to teaching and learning. The starting point is the amalgam of experiences, expectations and attributes of the students combined with the qualities of the tutor and the materials introduced. As already described, the learning sought can range from high-level abstract skills through to simple practical skills. Whatever the level, though, experiential learning needs to be well organised, carefully planned and perceived by students as purposeful.

If such criteria are satisfied then students can be motivated towards their own learning cycles. When this happens they are participating in a form of individual learning. This individuality, however, helps make the processes unpredictable. The responses of students, even to identical situations, will be variable. This is true for more transmissive teaching, but in experiential learning different reactions can be regarded as part of the learning experience. If students are disinclined to participate during a particular session this can provoke a learning cycle for both tutor and student, if the tutor has the skills to cope with and exploit the situation.

As with students, tutors learn at different rates. For some the notion of a learning community is difficult to accept. It seems to fly in the face of tradition and reality. They have to confront similar groups of students, day in, day out; year in, year out. The fact that each group is unique, and every student can be offered an individual learning cycle, seems insignificant compared with the tyranny of weekly timetables. Yet, often, the learning opportunities for tutors are greater than those for students, as they are more likely to be involved in similar situations again. The *Apply* stage of the learning cycle can have greater relevance in the context of their work.

Cynics may downgrade the emphasis on tutor learning. Such thinking is unfair. Effective tutors bring previous experience to bear upon the new learning situations in which they find themselves. Further experiences may influence (beneficially) still later situations. Successful tutors organise their own learning cycles. In this way they extend, modify and accelerate the learning of their students. To do so to effect, though, given the reality of timetables, they require access to good-quality material, and experience in using it. The nature of the material is covered later in the book.

It is not intended, however, to imply that all learning in schools and colleges should aim for an experiential mode. Transmissive teaching and experiential learning can be integrated successfully by both tutor and group. One topic is approached in a didactic manner, another seems more appropriately raised through the *Do, Review, Learn* and *Apply* model (see page 4). The skill of the tutor is to define appropriateness, relative to the expectations, preferences and negotiating skills of the group. The two approaches are not only able to coexist, they effectively reinforce each other.

A fundamental difference remains. Didactic teaching is mainly concerned with the transfer of knowledge and skills. Attention is focused on what skills and knowledge have been learned. Experiential learning concentrates upon the student and the processes of learning. The key questions here are about ways in which individual learning may be enriched and accelerated. Often the processes of learning ought to be more significant than the topic. Most frequently, though, issues related to what students learn dominate. This book tries to achieve a balance between topic and process. They are of equal importance.

2 Experiential learning and theory

Virtuous cycles

The learning of economic awareness (in the previous chapter) raises highly significant issues. On their own, a group of students would not often organise a formal learning cycle of *Do*, *Review*, *Learn* and *Apply*. Were they able to do so, a tutor would have no role. Few, if any, students would be aware of the notion of a learning cycle. None would be capable of articulating or describing it unprompted. Yet it cannot be denied that children begin to appreciate matters associated with economic awareness, like the place of money as a medium or exchange or the importance of a barter economy, at an early age. They will not use such terms but by the time they start school most children have learned some economic awareness. Such examples, and there are many more, of the power of ubiquitousness of experiential learning illustrate both its advantages and disadvantages.

According to Mumford (1984) a child who has learned some economic awareness has gone through a 'virtuous learning cycle'. The starting point – the effectiveness focus of the diagram (Figure 2.1) – may be a liking for sweets. The perceived relevance occurs when the association is made between access to money and the process of buying. An immediate application is possible if an adult (or another child) is persuaded to part with money. A reward follows when the sweets are acquired. Almost certainly there will be enthusiasm for further learning, both about associations between money and other desirable goods, and various techniques for cajoling or bribing parents to spend more money. Unwittingly (perhaps) adults have reinforced the virtuousness of the learning cycle, but all such activities happen without the supposed advantages of formal learning in school or college.

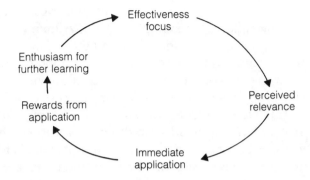

Figure 2.1 *The virtuous cycle*

Vicious cycles

Mumford goes on to draw a black contrast between a 'virtuous' and a 'vicious learning cycle'. This starts with a tutor defining an area of knowledge or skills which can be generalised. The intention is that this knowledge or these skills should be transferred to the students. It is then left to them to translate what they have learned from the transference processes to their own situations, possibly with some help from tutors. Not unexpectedly, many students will have difficulty in applying what the tutor wants them to learn to their own situations. Perhaps they fail to appreciate its relevence, or are not motivated towards that particular area of knowledge or skill. As a result they receive no rewards from the learning process, and in this particular context it may well cease. Also, enthusiasm for further learning in this, or possibly any other context, could be curtailed. Figure 2.2 outlines the process.

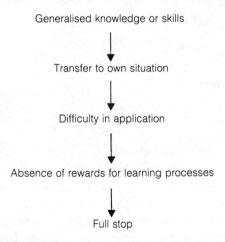

Figure 2.2 *The vicious cycle*

In many ways the comparison between the two cycles is unfair. The student (the young child in the example) is very well motivated towards economic awareness because of the desirable outcomes.

Conversely, a tutor faced with an externally imposed, knowledge-based syllabus would accept the first two stages of the vicious cycle, but see it as a prime duty to avoid, or at least remedy, the remaining stages. According to this view students will have difficulty in understanding transferred material and applying it to different situations, but a tutor ought to have the experience to overcome such problems. While student reward comes from possessing the knowledge or skills to pass an examination not all transmissive teaching leads to a vicious cycle.

Other cycles

One aspect of the contrast described above is apposite, however, and that is the different starting points of the two cycles. The virtuous cycle begins with a focus which the student regards as important. The vicious cycle starts with some knowledge or skills to be transferred. In fact all variants on an experiential learning cycle (and there are several) develop from some perception about student needs. So far, we have concentrated on the *Do, Review, Learn, Apply* model, but its relationship to the better-known cycle described by Kolb (1983) requires consideration (see Figure 2.3). The starting points are similar, with the *Do* stage replaced by Concrete Experience in Kolb's model. The reason for this is that the Kolb cycle tries to encompass a much greater range of learning situations than those constructed specifically within programmes or timetables of schools and colleges. Therefore an alternative starting point may be the actual experiences already acquired by course members, rather than some shared experience for all students organised by a tutor.

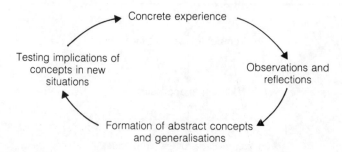

Figure 2.3 Kolb's cycle

Whatever form these experiences take, however, the second stage of each of the two cycles is described in a similar way. Instead of *Review* the students are given the opportunity to observe and reflect on their experiences. The resultant process can have a number of features. It may be a solitary activity, in which students write about their experiences, perhaps in preparation for discussing them with others. It could involve pairs of students questioning each other. Possibly it includes a period of reflection involving the whole group, during which students exchange perceptions about particular aspects of their experiences.

Tutors ought to have a crucial role in these activities. Essentially they must structure them so that not only do the processes themselves seem purposeful but, more significantly, individual students can appreciate how these purposes may relate to their own perceptions about needs. Only in this way will students feel committed to a learning cycle. As a result the balance that the tutor must appear to strike between group and individual interests becomes very important during this stage. The organisation or structure that a tutor suggests may take many shapes, but the observations and reflections, as well as the experiences on which they are based, remain unique to each student.

Likewise in the next step that Kolb describes – the formation of abstract concepts and generalisations (the *Learn* stage of the 'virtuous' cycle) – a tutor must aim for a balance between group concerns and the needs of the individual. Unless a student can generalise from previous experiences then there will be uncertainty about how to deal with new experiences, because each of them has certain unique features. Only when they understand relationships, through placing particular experiences in a wider context, can students learn to adapt their behaviour.

Central to this capacity to generalise is the formation of abstract concepts which enable a student to place actions, and their effects, in a framework based upon theory and empirical evidence. A tutor assists students to construct this framework. Indeed, throughout these stages of observation and generalisation the main task of the tutor is to facilitate students in collecting information about their experiences and then support them in its analysis. Students can assist, motivate and cajole each other substantially during these stages, but the individuality of the learning cycle remains immutable.

This becomes more obvious during the final stage of the cycle when it is suggested that students test the implications of the concepts they have abstracted and any generalisations they have made in new situations. More directly, if the learning cycle has been successful, a student has the capacity to act differently. As a result of previous experiences (some of which a tutor may have organised) and what has been learned from their analysis, students are capable of behaving in ways they would not have done, or did not know about, when confronted with new situations. They then test the implications of what has been learned in such situations. One learning cycle has been completed. However, another can begin and this may well happen more quickly and be more in line with a student's view of individual need because of what has been learned from previous cycles. Perceptions about success attract students towards more learning cycles.

As with the contrast between the 'virtuous' and the 'vicious' cycles, Kolb constructs an alternative pattern which can inhibit learning (Figure 2.4). On this occasion, though, the starting point is rather different. Instead of the generalised skill or knowledge of the 'vicious' cycle, it is the refusal by the potential learner to accept that a problem exists which begins the alternative cycle. Apparently the experiences of a student have not aroused awareness about a need to learn in this particular context.

As a result a tutor tries to organise a learning cycle but the student reflects that the learning alluded to is not important, or at most has to be of low priority. Even were a tutor to persuade the student to raise its priority, the conceptualisation stage might well be a feeling by the student that the problems associated with this learning cannot be solved. The student becomes convinced that the problem cannot be solved, and therefore does not experiment with alternative behaviour in new situations. With this chain of events there has been no attempt to construct a learning cycle, and perhaps there follows dimunition in confidence relative to other learning opportunities which may arise in the future.

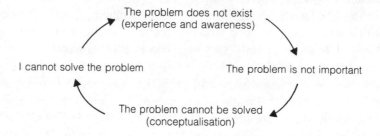

Figure 2.4 The alternative cycle

The role of the tutor

These cycles illustrate the many reasons why tutors can feel threatened by experiential learning. Sometimes they may wonder whether they have a role. They must contend with the ubiquitousness of experiential learning. This provides both an advantage (that every student has already proved capable of using learning cycles) and a disadvantage (that much of this use has occurred without the benefit of awareness). Students have become accustomed to learning in a whole range of natural settings but with little inkling of the formal stages that are available to categorise a learning cycle.

Students have done things (and had things done to them) when forming concrete experiences. They have reflected upon these events (maybe long afterwards). They have discussed them with colleagues, friends and family, and compared similar experiences. They have read and heard other media and comments. As a result they have generated and formulated their own concepts which have subsequently been tested. The problem for tutors is to help students further understand and refine these processes, without imposing constraints which inhibit students' willingness to construct their own cycles to cope with new materials and alternative situations.

Tutors can help formalise these learning processes in a school or college – but they cannot control them. If they organise a group experience, then what a student draws from it may be influenced but not directed by them. Often tutors do not possess detailed knowledge of the previous experiences or earlier learning of students and the ways these can interact with new experiences and the later stages of any intended cycle. Similarly, while they may well appreciate the individuality of the learning cycle, most tutors will still feel the need (quite appropriately) to try to motivate the activities and perceptions of perhaps 20 or 30 students. Invariably they will be inhibited in this part of their work by time constraints. Yet the students are doing no more – learning through their experiences – than they have become practised in (and perhaps reasonably skilled in) for most of their lives. It is not surprising that many tutors (and some outsiders) reflect upon whether a tutor has a proper function, other than provider of materials, time-keeper or custodian.

In practice, tutors do have an immensely important role. It is their task to accelerate and focus the learning processes. It is the familiarity with experiential learning that ought to make it so attractive to students and should provide its main advantage. However, without tutors there is not much chance to raise students' awareness towards this familiarity. Tutors may do this through discussion so that previous learning cycles can be illuminated. They may achieve the same end through example, for there is no more effective means of boosting confidence and raising enthusiasm than the successful completion of a learning cycle. Where appropriate, tutors have a responsibility to provide suitable materials and ideas.

However much they encourage familiarity, though, tutors can only fulfil their role with the agreement of an individual student. They cannot speed the learning process, and they cannot shape the support processes of experience, reflection, conceptualisation, etc unless the student accepts the objectives sought and thinks that the processes to be adopted are a suitable way to achieve them. In a broad sense, perhaps the most difficult task for tutors is to convince students of any need to learn.

In the context of development Dubin (1962) introduces the neat concept of two dichotomies – one between those students that require some particular learning and those that possess it already, and another between those who are aware of what they do not know and those who are not. Diagrammatically this produces four categories of student (Figure 2.5). Their respective attitudes to learning have been added.

The task of a tutor is to maintain a state of 'conscious incompetence' (awareness of the need to learn a particular knowledge or skill) among as many students as possible. If most students start from a position of unconscious incompetence about a topic, the first job of a tutor is to assist them to become conscious of their incompetence. Students are then in a position to learn. If they learn, they become conscious and competent and therefore both confident (because of the success of the earlier learning) and conscious of what else they may need to learn.

However, as the next section discusses, this is no easy task. It can indeed be a threatening one given the many different needs even of a fairly cohesive group of students, and the varied experiences (including those in learning) to which the students have been subjected.

Competent relative to a particular skill or knowledge	Unconscious competence (not interested in this particular learning)	Conscious competence (requiring learning in new areas)
Incompetent	Unconscious incompetence (in need of learning but unaware of the need)	Conscious incompetence (very suitable for learning)
	Unconscious of a need to learn a particular skill or knowledge	Conscious

Figure 2.5 Dubin's dichotomies

The needs of students

Perhaps the greatest challenge posed to tutors, if they are to satisfy the needs of most of their students, is the very individuality of those needs. To a large extent this issue is overlooked in the didactic mode. It is assumed that all students to whom knowledge or skills are to be transferred have need of them. If not, there is no point in their belonging to the class. Experiential learning, by starting with the specific experiences of each student and using these to construct a unique learning style, is trying to provide individualised learning but within a group setting.

It does not follow that individualisation ought to incline students to individual working; the interactions among students may well provide the most significant aspects of all parts of the learning cycle. Nor do the demands of the group imply that the programme for every student, as structured by a tutor, must be identical. Clearly such an arrangement would make a nonsense of any need to cater for the varied needs and experiences of a group of students.

At no stage of the cycle is this more obvious than with *Review*. Students cannot be made to reflect. They may be offered a common experience. Alternatively, a tutor may suggest that students would like the opportunity to consider some earlier experiences. The students may accept the opportunity, but in many cases their willingness to do so will be highly dependent upon the environment and the mechanisms contrived by the tutor. Schon (1987), writing about professional development, sees the chance to consider and analyse as a key concept in the attainment of the reflective practitioner. In a busy life of continuous demands and increasing accountability the only way that a professional person may achieve growth and self-renewal is through some processes of systematic reflection. Without these processes, the individual professional and the clients must be disadvantaged.

Some professionals have the capacity for unsupported reflection but most require some assistance, perhaps with a tutor working alongside a peer group. Between them, if successful, they can demonstrate the need for learning (the incompetence element) and raise awareness about the need (the consciousness factor). More significantly, as the demands of professional life continue to change, they can convince the practitioner of the necessity of developing habits which sustain a constant state of reflectiveness.

A similar principle is appropriate for a less mature student audience. Achieving a readiness to be reflective about experiences and to learn from those experiences, so that they may influence future behaviour, is as important to them as it is for professional staff. Their immaturity, though, adds a further dimension. It makes different demands upon the tutor. A professional is better placed to define needs, and make judgements about their satisfaction. With less mature students the role of the tutor may have to be more intrusive.

More significantly a particular emphasis in a tutor's work with professional staff must be to concentrate upon consciousness relative to particular facets of competence. This aspect is important for other groups also, but if professionals remain unconvinced about a tutor's capacity to assist them their non-participation will be signified by withdrawal. This may be disturbing for both tutor and 'professional' student but it at least avoids the situation, which can occur with a school or college group, where some students are active participants while others display little interest. At worst they may try to disrupt the experiences, observations and discussion of others. Such students can be located at any of the four quadrants shown in Figure 2.5 on page 22. Their backgrounds of knowledge, skills, motivation and previous exposure to experiential learning will vary widely. There will be no consistency among their priorities.

Within the same group a tutor can find students who know a good deal about the issue under scrutiny but wish to know more, that is, conscious but willing to explore their levels of incompetence. Next to them may be students who are unaware that they know little and remain unconcerned (content with their unconsciousness and incompetence) whatever actions a tutor takes.

In one respect, though, a tutor and a less mature group offer considerable flexibility. Argyris (1982) contrasts single and double-loop learning. Single-loop learning occurs when individuals can satisfy a particular learning need, without the necessity of reviewing the basic values that induced the original learning requirements. A student acquires some knowledge or skill, but the underlying factors which may have contributed to the deficiency receive little or no attention. In these circumstances the various elements of the learning cycle have not been fully exercised.

In double-loop learning, it is argued, more fundamental issues are considered, perhaps leading to modification of some basic values that constrain behaviour. The process of reflection has been more significant. Wider generalisations may have been attempted, and a broader range of new actions tested. Often a less mature group, with fewer inhibitions, are more attracted to double-loop learning than moderately reflective professionals who simply want to acquire some new knowledge or skill which might be useful at the margins of performance. A tutor can assist the latter to be adventurous and self-inquiring about motives so that the double-loop can reinforce their learning cycles.

Learning styles

So far no attention has been paid to a further potential difference among students – that they each have a preferred learning style. In a didactic mode this is not significant. The assumption is that if a tutor translates the material to the students adequately, and if the material meets the students' requirements, then learning will follow. The appropriateness of the assumption may be tested, where necessary, by an examination. There may be some consideration of whether students prefer 'handout' or guided reading, or of how much they may appreciate the use of visual aids, but resultant choices represent some consensus about the group preference. By force of circumstance, the group view must supercede a whole range of individual preferences from which it has evolved. Experiential learning, if it is to realise its potential, cannot afford the luxury of ignorance. Because it is predicated upon the notion of students constructing unique learning cycles, it cannot ignore individuals' preferences about their own learning styles.

Accepting this idea, though, poses two formidable problems for tutors. First there is the idiosyncracity of every student, even within a relatively small group. They learn at different rates. They have varied educational backgrounds. They hold many expectations and as many views about whether a particular educational experience and tutor is likely to realise these expectations. They each possess inherent traits and a unique personality profile. In addition, it is now being inferred that everyone has a characteristic learning style. The collection of variables that a tutor may consider appears almost endless.

Second, if a tutor is to make any practical use of this issue of learning styles there has to be some process of classification. Such a process, though, is fraught with difficulty. Not only is each individual's style unique, within that uniqueness experience tells us that our own preferences depend on circumstances. They are affected by topic, commitment to it, previous experiences with a particular group, the environment of the learning and so on. To return to an example mentioned in the previous chapter, a student may have a clear preference about how to learn to repair a television (to see a programme next day) but a rather different preference towards assertiveness training, because of comments about what may be involved in that training made by previous students.

Notwithstanding these difficulties, Honey and Mumford (1982), after a number of years of empirical work, proposed that four predominant styles existed, and that preferences regarding them can be assessed quite easily.

1 *Activists* are interested in novelty. They are willing to become involved in new experiences, and are content to be dominated by more immediate experiences. As a result they are attracted by different ideas, alternative approaches and novel ways of performing tasks or organising work. Often they are incautious, and revel in moving from one situation to another as the opportunity arises. This aspect of the new means that they tend to give insufficient attention to the implications, for themselves and for others, when they embark on new arrangements to which they are easily attracted. Alternative experiences provide challenges on which they thrive, but they become bored with (for example) implementing a new scheme, when their initial enthusiasm wanes.

2 *Reflectors* are determined that they must have time to think about new

experiences or ideas when they confront them. They are cautious when presented with material they have not met before. They like to consider it from as many perspectives as possible. They will not draw conclusions without a full opportunity to collect as much evidence as possible, or discover all the facts that seem available. Without the available information, and the chance to reflect upon it, they are reluctant to draw conclusions, and therefore can be perceived as indecisive. They watch and listen to others before expressing their views and, overall, tend to adopt a low profile.

3 *Theorists* are most concerned about linkages and relationships. When presented with new material they wish to fit it into an overall framework, and find it difficult to assimilate such material unless they can appreciate how it matches with or supports concepts they already hold. They try to think problems through in a logical way, and are only satisfied with coherent theories. Both analysis and synthesis attract, which can make them appear detached and keen to reject ambiguities. In general they pursue strategies that help them understand the interactions between all components of a particular issue.

4 *Pragmatists* are driven by a need to ensure that any new material they encounter can be applied in practice. They want to know if an idea or a technique will work. Their main attention, therefore, is towards relevance. Unless they can envisage some way in which knowledge or a skill can be used it is of little interest to them. However, they want to act quickly on new ideas that attract them. A main purpose of their learning is satisfaction of their need to solve problems which are important to them. They are interested in arrangements that work, and are therefore concerned with practicalities.

Honey and Mumford do not suggest that everyone falls naturally into one category to the exclusion of others. We have a preference, they claim, towards activism, reflection, theorism or pragmatism. To assess the extent of this preference, the authors devised an 80-item questionnaire (with 20 statements for each of the categories).

So, for example, the 'activist' category includes the statement:
I enjoy being the one that talks a lot.
Respondents are asked to tick this if they agree more than they disagree, or cross it if they disagree more than they agree.

For reflectors, a similar statement is:
If I have a report to write, I tend to produce lots of drafts before settling on the final version.

For theorists:
In discussions with people I often find I am the most dispassionate and objective.

And for pragmatists:

In discussions I often find I am the realist, keeping people to the point and avoiding 'cloud nine' speculations.

When results are totalled, students finish with a profile (Figure 2.6) which can be compared with both national norms and scores for different groups.

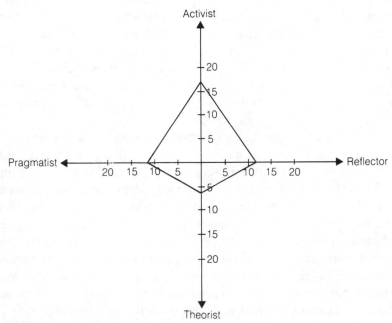

Figure 2.6 A typical profile

The Honey and Mumford classification provides a tool for the tutor; it offers further information which can influence the design of experiential learning programmes. However, it is a very crude tool, strongly affected by the individual perceptions of students and the ways in which they interpret arbitrary statements and apply them to hypothetical situations. Even with the deficiencies, though, it can be used to assist students consider their own learning. They may discuss in small groups their own score, and how they feel it relates to their own perceptions of learning behaviour. The role of fellow group members as outsiders can be crucial because they can offer their observations about behaviour in a new learning situation and how this behaviour might have been anticipated from the questionnaire scores. Strategies can be devised which take into account student preferences when they wish to learn some new material or a different skill.

All that the Honey and Mumford classification tries to do is clarify some features of learning preferences for individual students. Most find they score above average on one or perhaps two categories. A few score very highly on one range and feel attracted to the attributes described.

Some have an average profile, and seem well capable of reinforcing a balanced learning style. Ways in which more students may achieve this state of affairs are considered more fully in the next chapter.

There is always some risk attached to the use of such instruments. Students who score highly in one category may be inclined to think that all their learning ought to demonstrate the characteristics associated with that category. The high-scoring 'reflector' becomes even more reflective, and so on. In other words, the test has served to reinforce and perhaps overstrengthen one aspect of learning. If this happens, of course, the three remaining categories stand to receive too little attention. The 'reflector's' inclination to activism and willingness to participate in new experiences is reduced, and the student may be more reluctant to consider the practical implications of alternative materials or approaches because of a low rating as a pragmatist.

There is always a possibility of students misusing or abusing such instruments. This can happen with individuals or in a group setting, and sometimes tutors can unwittingly contribute to it. The main learning comes from the opportunities offered to students to interpret some external advice, supported by empirical evidence, about their own preferences. Completion of the questionnaire and subsequent discussion, therefore, constitutes another learning cycle. Undoubtedly the function of other members of the learning community is of enormous significance. The intention is to assist students to interpret this additional information about themselves in the context of previous learning and planning for (and attitudes towards) new learning.

What the Honey and Mumford classification reaffirms, even with the caveats discussed, is the student-centredness of experiential learning. In this case attention is redirected towards the learning style of the individual, with the intention that this will expedite learning. As such it represents a blend of self and external feedback. The relationship between the two is best demonstrated through the use of a Johari's window (Luft, 1970) as show in Figure 2.7. One dimension (horizontal) is concerned for the information students hold about their views, attitudes and feelings; it has two elements – that information of which students are aware (known to self) and that of which they are unaware (unknown to self). The second dimension considers the same information held by students but here concern focuses upon the awareness of others. The divide along this axis is between the information students transmit to others and that which students deliberately withhold from others. The outcome is a square with four rectangular blocks.

One result of successful experiential learning is to permit students to expand block 3 (see Figure 2.7). They thus have a greater awareness of the extent to which they demonstrate their own views, attitudes and feelings through behaviour. They have learned to reduce block 4, in that they possess more knowledge of what others might infer from their

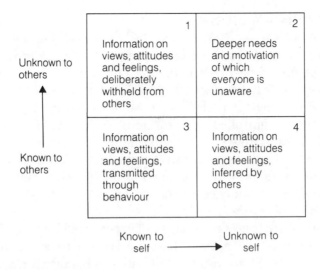

Figure 2.7 The Johari window

behaviour. At the same time they have become more conscious of what they withhold or reveal to others (contracting block 1) and to some extent they may also have become more alert to deeper needs and motives represented by block 2, so that too is smaller (Figure 2.8). Tutors and other students, as part of the learning community, can assist one another in exploring the issues raised by this model, and how they can be related to the construction of learning cycles. It can provide another element in the consideration of learning styles.

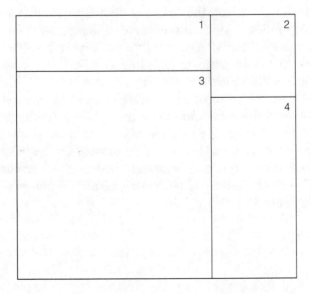

Figure 2.8 Changes in the Johari window resulting from experiential learning

An over-reliance on theory

Human learning is far too complex a process to give us broad theories which might help us explain or predict outcomes. It is impossible to prove or disprove hypotheses with empirical evidence covering a broad range of educational activities. The variables involved are just too numerous to be controlled or measured. Yet if the activities under consideration are narrowed to limit the number of variables, clearly it would be most unwise to generalise from the results obtained. Such comments apply to both experiential and more transmissive modes of learning. There is no evidence to establish experiential learning as better, nor would any be expected.

Similarly there is no single theory of experiential learning, but there are several theories which try to describe various aspects of it. In this context the notion of learning cycles provides an important contribution. They can be used to most effect by tutors when designing programmes, for what they are doing then is to help students expedite and shape their own learning styles. Some student awareness about cycles offers a number of potential benefits if individual students can perceive how the various stages relate to what they are trying to learn. However, for both tutors and students to concentrate too much on the cycles will prove counter-productive.

There must be a twin focus on the 'how' and the 'what' of the learning. If too much emphasis is placed upon the *processes* of learning and items like preferred styles, or evaluation and feedback, then students will learn little. Sometimes they can be attracted to these processes, particularly as they apply to themselves, but unless there is concern for the 'what' of the learning these processes soon become viewed as purposeless. For example, some students may want to develop more economic awareness. As a result a tutor may be able to interest them in how they can learn to be more economically aware, and be extremely successful. Further learning about a wholly different topic may be expedited. Thus economic awareness has been used as a twin vehicle: relative both to economics and the students' learning processes. Learning about learning, for its own sake, attracts very few students.

Conversely, didactic styles can be dominated by the 'what' and pay minimal attention to the 'how' – as reflected in the learning needs of students. The most effective experiential learning achieves a 'how' and 'what' relationship.

3 The behaviour of the learners

The what–how balance

If experiential learning is to build upon the previous learning experiences of students it must avoid the appearance of artificiality. Students have learned much in natural surroundings. The challenge for the tutor is to harness and refine the learning skills that students have already acquired. If the processes of experiential learning are to be shaped and speeded by the tutor then the naturalness of these requires protection. This will not happen if the notion of the learning cycle receives too much attention. An example would be when the various stages of the cycle, and what students ought to be doing about them at any time, are explained laboriously and repeatedly to students.

In practice, the steps of the cycle frequently overlap and are inseparable:

- A tutor organises an experience for the students – they *Do*.
- Time is then set aside for analysis and discussion of the experience – they *Review*.
- The tutor then introduces some theory or suggests a generalisation – they *Learn*.
- Ideas or recommendations about how the learning might be tried or tested are considered – they *Apply*.

Written like this, and reinforced by the diagrammatic representations of the learning cycles, four discrete steps are implied. In reality nothing could be further from the truth.

Most students are perfectly capable of *Doing* and *Reviewing* simultaneously. They may well have generalised about an experience before a tutor attempts to offer insights, or decided how they are going to try out some new learning ahead of any tutor-led discussions about the application stage. Invariably, students will not think of new behaviour in narrow terms of it having to be tested first before they embark on another learning cycle, because they have become accustomed to dealing with a number of learning cycles simultaneously.

In anything tutors organise, numerous learning cycles are likely. It would be unwise to attempt to stifle them, even were this feasible. As already mentioned, students learn at their own pace in an individualistic manner. The process can be influenced by a tutor, but it cannot be controlled. To expect that every student must go at the same rate around an identical learning cycle, as organised by the tutor, is wrong.

If tutors structure sessions so that it appears they insist upon this expectation, they endanger some aspects of the learning, not least those associated with student motivation. Yet little learning intended by tutors will result if they leave their sessions unstructured or do not appear to plan. The students will perceive this as purposelessness, and attitudes towards their own learning will be hindered rather than helped.

Despite the drawbacks, the idea of the cycle is invaluable, because that is how experiential learning appears to happen. It ought to be a significant concept for tutors because it helps them think through the most appropriate ways of organising the time they spend with students.

It does not follow, though, that space has to be found for each stage in every individual session. Sometimes a timetable demands that the *Do* and group *Review* stages must be separated by several days, although this will detract from the *Learning*. It would lead to even more inflexibility were it assumed that sessions ought to be divided into four equal lengths and that the stage students are supposed to have reached must be explained at every opportunity.

Tutors should be able to enlighten students about the learning cycle they are organising, but they cannot know (at the time) the other cycles students are constructing. As students gain maturity they can become much more aware of the notion of a cycle (with tutors' assistance), what it may be able to offer them, and how they may make use of it when organising their own learning. Understandably, they are more interested in the what of learning. However, if a balance is achieved, and they become concerned about the how, it makes future learning far more attractive.

Styles and stages of learning

A major criticsim of any learning model is the difficulty in reconciling the neat outline of what is (or ought to be) happening with practical realities. This is particularly the case for experiential learning models. They do no more than describe behaviour. However, they can help both tutors and students understand how their behaviour influences learning.

One way in which this happens is best illustrated through the links between the learning cycle and learning styles. Someone with an activist preference is most attracted by the *Do* stage of the cycle. They welcome new experiences. They tend to regard them as opportunities to learn. The activities themselves, with their 'here and now' dimension, seem appealing and also provide a chance to gain attention from other group members.

By contrast a preference for the reflector role suggests students best suited for the *Review* stage. Here they can watch the actions of others and have time to think. They are enabled to reflect on what they have learned. There may be few time constraints for making decisions. They can determine their own priorities about the learning intended during this stage.

Students who score most highly as theorists are pulled towards the third stage of the cycle. Here, they are encouraged to make associations between previous pieces of learning, and then look for inter-relationships so that they can fit new learning into an established framework. In this way they can understand the generalisations which are so important to them. They are, also, most likely to be intellectually stretched during this stage and this they also find attractive.

High-scoring pragmatists are most interested in discovering whether recently-acquired knowledge or skills have practical applications. It is the fourth stage of the cycle that they find most appealing. At this point the links between the material covered and possible uses are sought. Students can concentrate on the practical matters of whether something they have learned will work. They can try out newly acquired knowledge or techniques, and then be in a position to receive feedback about how successful they have been.

Honey (1984) continued by suggesting key questions for each preference.

For activists:
Shall I learn something new or something I could not do before?
Will there be many things for me to do?
Shall I be able to work with people like myself?
Will I be able to regard the learning opportunity as a challenge?

For reflectors:
Shall I have sufficient time to think about any new material?
Will there be opportunity to collect more information, if necessary, so that I can clarify issues?
Shall I be given the opportunity to hear the views of others?
Will these views be from a variety of people?

For theorists:
Will there be opportunities to ask questions?

Will the objectives and the activities planned have a clear structure and purpose?
Shall I meet complex ideas so that I am stretched intellectually?
Are the approaches to be adopted sound?

For pragmatists:
Will there be opportunity to try out whatever is learned?
Will there be time to consider practical techniques?
Shall we be considering real problems which are relevant to me?
Will I be able to use what I learn?

The intention of such questions is not to divide students into four distinct categories. Instead it is to help them understand their own learning. If a student leans too heavily towards one preference then his or her learning capacity will be blunted. For example, a pragmatist may reject anything which does not appear to have a fairly immediate application, or an activist may be too inclined to move from one idea to the next as attention switches, without fully appreciating any underlying theory.

These examples are extremes, but tutors must be cautious that students do not feel forced to make characterisations of themselves based on learning preferences. Most students have a preference for one or two styles, but not to the exclusion of the others. Tutors can use questions of this type to stimulate individuals or groups of students. They should relate to what students expect to gain from particular sessions. They can help to harness interests, and also focus some of the activities, as tutors prompt students to ask such questions about their involvement. In this way their commitment to any learning can be enhanced.

Students' learning capabilities

A considerable attraction of giving time to preferred learning cycles is the obvious commitment made towards student responsibility for learning. It not only demonstrates to students their individuality but – more significantly – it asks them to consider how they learn. This is not an abstract question. If presented as such by tutors it will put most students off any further consideration. However, all students are interested in themselves; if this feature can be developed it provides an effective motivational force. The main problem for most tutors is overcoming the accompanying organisational difficulties.

At the core of the problem is student individuality. Tutors work with groups. Even the simplest calculations reveal the relatively short time that a tutor can spend with one student, in the course of a normal teaching timetable. Time shortage can be used to justify adopting a didactic mode of teaching. As a result students will be told what they ought to know about learning cycles. Such an approach has two drawbacks. First, while the students may be able to memorise a good deal about learning cycles as a result, that is only part of the desired outcome. It is their capacity to understand, apply the learning when appropriate and transfer it to new situations, which constitute far more significant attributes. Until they progress through these levels of learning, as described in the next section, students do not possess an adequate knowledge of learning cycles.

The second drawback of the approach is that it tries to offer all students the same knowledge, when their relative states of development are certain to be different. Among group members there will be similarities of learning capabilities, but there will be many more, and much greater, variations. The main task of the tutor is to help students become aware of their own capabilities and how these can be enhanced. Sometimes a tutor may identify a contrast in learning preferences between two students that helps both of them. Group discussions may be helpful in exploring issues. The learning cycle is a model which appeals more to some students than others, but it is often useful in raising awareness. Its use to structure sessions offers students an added experience about the cycle, and the related guidance tutors can give (to individuals and groups) should make them more alert to their own learning.

Learning cycles structured by tutors are important for two main reasons. First, they may be useful in helping students learn about the topic planned for a particular session. Second, and more significantly, there is the possibility of transfer: in the process of participating in this cycle students have gained in their knowledge of how they might learn more successfully about other topics elsewhere. When this happens they have become more capable learners.

However, these are processes unique to an individual. When they are wholly successful a tutor's role does become irrelevant. Even as these processes occur, with the students achieving varying success, some tutors can perceive themselves as redundant. When this happens they are easily enticed to return to a more transmissive style of teaching. Yet they still have a vital role to play. No student is ever wholly successful, so that he or she has nothing more to learn. Some may think that this is the case, on occasion, or believe it is not worth learning any more about a particular topic, or that a tutor cannot help them, but essentially these are motivational issues.

The most important challenge to a tutor is to raise the learning capabilities of students. This means assisting students to consider how they learn most effectively. It involves helping them discuss their individual preferences about learning. Students will not be motivated towards such activities if they seem to occur in a vacuum. Activities need to be related to the learning of topics and issues which are of concern to the students. By this means students experience real achievement. As a result they become more confident. Enthusiasm for further learning is engendered and if tutors fulfil their roles they have additional interests in the learning process.

However, to attain these ends tutors need to be conscious of their own motivational patterns, and how their learning preferences might affect the activities they organise and the attitudes they convey to a group. Students quickly become aware of the attitudes, enthusiasms, dislikes and confidence of tutors. If tutors are to be appreciated as members of the learning community, students need to be able to perceive them as learning too.

Tutors are poorly equipped to raise the learning capabilities of students if they lack awareness of their own capabilities and how these might be increased.

Levels of learning

Tutors helping students towards more effective learning behaviour have a difficult task. Quite possibly the experiential learning they plan for students involves each of the four domains of Bloom's taxonomy – psychomotor, cognitive, affective and interpersonal. Only when the purpose of a session is narrow – for example learning a technique (in sport perhaps) or how to use a machine for a specific task – are considerations focused on one domain, in this case the psychomotor. In experiential learning the domains often overlap; this is even more likely in the learning cycles that students are able to construct around the main one which a tutor has used to organise the session.

Even when they try to clarify their learning processes students are unlikely to focus on domains. They are much more interested in levels of learning which can be applied to each of the domains. There are four:

1 *Memory*   A student is able to memorise some knowledge or technique and is able to reproduce it.

2 *Understanding* A student understands the knowledge or technique, is capable of explaining it, and sees the relationship between this material and a broader framework of knowledge.

3 *Application*   At this level a student can apply the knowledge or technique in a limited range of situations, probably with the aid of someone more experienced.

4 *Transfer*   By this stage a student can not only apply what has been learned but is now in a position to make judgements about other situations (some of which

have never been encountered before) where the transfer of knowledge and its application may be of value.

There is no reason why the transfer level must always be pursued. Students may only want to know how to use a screwdriver, without being interested in the principle of moments or the law of levers. Similarly students may require an understanding of quadratic equations; they could even have to apply that knowledge, but have no wish for a transfer level of understanding. In one respect the levels further complicate the role of tutors. In any group, almost certainly, students will define their learning needs at different levels, even for the same topic.

Some students will also find it much easier than others to proceed through memory and understanding to the later levels. These processes of student differentiation can be further exaggerated by learning preferences. Pragmatists, for example, are most likely to accept memorising a topic, if they feel that this satisfies a particular need. Theorists, however, even with the same superficial requirements (to pass an examination, perhaps) are still likely to be attracted to later levels of learning.

Effective learning behaviour

Tutor knowledge of levels is useful in defining objectives and discussing with students their learning intentions. It provides another element in efforts to help them understand their own capabilities in relation to what they want to learn. Undeniably, though, students must go through learning cycles in which their sensitivity to levels, preferences and needs is raised before they are enabled to shape and accelerate more cycles.

Sometimes it is difficult for a tutor to ascertain whether students are participants, or even interested, in issues related to their own learning. They may be quiet and unreactive. Not all will take part in discussions or be willing to answer questions from tutors and group members. There are many explanations for such silence – lack of confidence, uncertainty as to how others will react to comments or inability to articulate clearly – as well as the most obvious: that students are not interested. In the context of learning, enthusiasm follows confidence which, in turn, is established through achievement. As tutors persuade students that they have been successful, they are motivated to become even more effective learners. To do so they must refine some specific skills, and Mumford (1982) suggests they can be divided into 14 categories:

1 The ability to establish your own effectiveness criteria.
2 The ability to measure your effectiveness.

3 The ability to identify your own learning needs.
4 The ability to plan your own learning.
5 The ability to use learning opportunities.
6 The ability to review your own learning processes.
7 The ability to listen to others.
8 The capacity to seek out and accept help.
9 The ability to confront any unwelcome information.
10 The ability to take risks and accept uncertainties.
11 The ability to observe the learning of others.
12 The ability to learn about yourself.
13 The ability to share information and receive feedback.
14 The ability to review what has been learned.

The range is comprehensive. To present it, as it stands, to all but the maturest of students, would achieve nothing. Indeed it might well prove counter-productive, because it seems to imply a series of artificial divides within processes which occur naturally. A tutor might plan a session with the intention of assisting students become better listeners or more able to get help from other students, but many other skills could also be refined during the session, depending upon the students and the environment. The tutor would be unwise to inhibit those parallel learning processes, even were this practicable. They are part of the 'messiness' of experiential learning.

The skills associated with effective learning behaviour do not represent some sort of checklist, to be pursued individually in a series of sessions. If they are perceived in this way by students it will reduce their enthusiasm for the experiential mode. The main interest of students remains firmly with the topic – the 'what' of learning. Their concern for the 'how', when it can be separated from the 'what', is generally minimal. That is not to say they have no inclination towards effective learning behaviour. The great majority can be very favourably inclined towards it, provided it seems able to help them learn more quickly and easily about those topics in which they have an interest.

Tutor responsibilities

The normal institutional constraints of buildings, resources, timetables etc notwithstanding, tutors have responsibility for the following elements in the learning environment:

- The topic, knowledge or skill to be pursued (although the precise nature may involve negotiation with students);
- The resources and materials available;
- The previous learning sought with those students (both content and process);

- The time to be made available;
- Their own learning and tutoring style preferences.

They have a measure of control over these elements by whatever means they choose to exercise it. However, they can only influence (sometimes to little effect) the preferred learning styles of their students and significant learning attributes such as their motivation, interests and ability. These factors introduce additional complexity into individual learning and tutors can be assisted by further knowledge about learning processes. Bruner (1971), for example, argues that there are three main ways in which students convert their experiences so as to construct models of the world:

1 Through actions – from the senses of touching, handling and other physical activity.
2 Through images – from the build-up of images in their own minds which does not involve physical contact with objects.
3 Through the use of symbols – learning through words, language and mathematical concepts. In this last mode symbols have taken over from images, which have previously replaced physical involvement.

Experiential learning can involve all three forms of converting experiences into models of the world. Perhaps the *Doing* or the concrete experience stage includes physical actions. At all stages it is highly likely that students will build images, and tutors may want to encourage these processes, not necessarily in terms of constructing a specific image of an experience, but more generally through building models which can then be associated with further experiences or knowledge which tutors anticipate that students will acquire later.

Students also use symbols throughout the learning cycle, most particularly in the later stages when they attempt to generalise or consider how they may extend what they have learned into new situations. Indeed symbols prove invaluable in persuading students to discuss their experiences and make conceptual links between these and knowledge, materials and ideas raised by other group members and tutors.

While some tutors find the complexities of the learning process challenging, others find them a disincentive. Perhaps they think they already know sufficient to enable them to do their jobs competently. Possibly they feel that so complex are the processes of human learning, so idiosyncratic the learning needs, previous experiences, intellectual capacity and personality features for every student, that what one of them learns, and how this occurs, can be regarded almost as a matter of chance. Such views represent a total surrender to the messiness of experiential learning. They are incompatible also with membership of the learning community and will soon be spotted by many students.

Yet these attitudes on the part of tutors are also not unknown in relation to more didactic styles of teaching. In both contexts they arise mainly from the impenetrabilities associated with understanding human learning, but the absence (usually) of any form of systematic staff appraisal provides a significant contributory factor.

Tutor performance

Lack of interest in appraising the performance of tutors is long-standing. One explanation lies in the problems involved in evaluating performance. Tutors have a difficult job. They are unable to control the learning of their students, they can only influence the learning activities. The problems of assessing student outcomes (what they have learned) are substantial; but they are much less and more solvable than those involved in estimating a tutor's contribution to what a student has learned.

However, to concentrate upon these judgemental aspects of appraisal reduces the significance of its developmental potential. For tutors the role of appraisal as a potential tool to aid staff development is a much more important issue than simple judgements about good, moderate or bad performances. Indeed, appraisal should be the point around which development activity is focused. Tutors cannot be developed until they have been appraised.

An effective appraisal system should offer tutors a major learning opportunity. They have the chance of constructing learning cycles relative to their own personal and professional development, and ought to have the assistance of colleagues in those processes. Appraisal can demonstrate essential features of a learning community by encouraging tutors to reflect upon their strengths (and how these could be used to greater effect) while considering any weaknesses (and means by which these might be remedied).

Tutors should be able to discuss their satisfactions and frustrations about the work alongside other factors like the availability of resources, or the level of institutional support. The actual arrangements may take many forms. A number of practical matters require attention: Who should carry out appraisal interviews (who should appraise whom)? What ought to be the nature of the documentation? Should the tutors be observed working with students (if so, by whom, and on what basis) etc?

Such practical difficulties are surmountable, as already demonstrated by some schools and colleges, but they will confirm many tutors' views about the messiness of this particular component of their experiential learning. No matter how well-organised the procedures, and how competently staff perform their appraising tasks, some tutors will resent what they regard as intrusions into their work. They may not appreciate the developmental functions of appraisal, and believe it to be totally concerned with judgements (invariably adverse) about their own performance. They may resent the 'institutionalisation' of private procedures they have participated in for some time. When such attitudes emerge among tutors, the appraisal system has failed. It has not reinforced the interest of tutors in their own development, and the mechanisms by which their learning can be further shaped and accelerated.

More specifically in the context of experiential learning, appraisal has also failed when it is not used as an opportunity to clarify the role of individual tutors. On occasion, tutors need to discuss what they are trying to achieve with groups of students, especially when so much of the achievement is intangible. They want the school or college to understand their difficulties. From a professional stand-point they must be aware of the complexities of student learning, but if too much about this complexity is transmitted to students it is unlikely to interest them and may well be counter-productive in inhibiting the 'naturalness' of experiential learning on which so much of the subsequent activity is to be based.

Tutors have a key role in experiential learning, but usually it is difficult to define their actions. As a result they can find it hard to describe what they do. Normally it is impossible to assess their specific contributions to student achievement. As a counter measure to these uncertainties, words such as facilitator, enlightener, motivator, clarifier or provider are sometimes used to describe the role of tutors. These are of little significance, and do not help tutors who are trying to justify a role. Nor do they offer much guidance about the most appropriate tutor behaviour in given circumstances.

Appraisal for development purposes, if appropriately organised, can assist tutors enormously in working out the best contributions they can make. Of course it is possible (if not probable) that if appraisal is forced upon tutors by legislation, and the model adopted is perceived as hierarchical and 'top-down', many of the potential benefits will not be achieved. Appraisal will be viewed as a tool of management, to be used to reward or punish, and it will contribute little to the development of appropriate tutors' skills and attitudes.

What cannot be denied about experiential learning, when tutors and students regard it as successful, is the key role of the tutor in assisting students consider their own learning behaviour, how this might be enhanced, and the beneficial effects that can result in future learning situations. There are limits and constraints to achieving these ends, however, and they will be discussed in the next chapter.

4 Experiential learning as a motivator

Learning capacities

Because experiential learning tries to build upon natural learning processes, it can appeal to a wide range of ages, abilities and student interests when introduced into an institutional context. As an approach it can be used with quite young children in one context and, by contrast, in the development of senior professional staff elsewhere. Age and intellectual capacity need not be barriers to learning cycles. They affect learning needs and capacities, but not the universality of the cycle. Indeed it would be quite remiss to suspect that one learning cycle can be described for adults, another for children. That is why the contrast Knowles (1984) draws between two distinct patterns for learning: pedagogy and andragogy, must be accepted with some caution.

Five differences are itemised by Knowles on the assumption that pedagogy involves a transmissive teaching mode (most appropriate to pupils) while androgogy describes a pattern more in tune with the needs of the adult learner. These differences are:

1 *The learner concept* In pedagogy the student is assumed to be a dependent learner with the tutor responsible for determining the material, the method and the timing of the learning, as well as the assessment of whether learning has occurred. The contrast here is between the pedagogic learner – accepting procedures controlled by the tutor – and the andragogic learner – who is more self-directed, and has a measure of responsibility for deciding the most appropriate learning arrangements.

2 *The learner's previous experiences* With a pedagogical approach it is assumed that the learner has little previous experience either about the topic or in learning methods. The tutor is therefore translating material to the student who ought to be in a position to accept it, if the

tutor's judgement is correct. Earlier learning experiences are not regarded as particularly relevant. In an andragogical approach, however, the previous experiences of the learners are allowed to assume a more significant role not only because they provide a base of knowledge or skill, but also they can be useful in determining the rate and means by which new material is most appropriately assimilated.

3 *Learning readiness* In a pedagogical environment, decisions about whether students are ready to learn a particular topic remain the responsibility of the tutor and are largely determined by the age of the student and modified by other timetable constraints. Andragogically, students influence, or may even 'control', such decisions when they perceive a need to know. It is they who determine learning priorities. In practice a tutor can alter that perception by helping students become aware of a deficiency or persuading them to reconsider their priorities, but it is assumed that students will not be in a position to learn until they have decided they are willing.

4 *Organisation of the material* The notion of pedagogy is most usually linked with the prevailing curriculum orthodoxy of schools and colleges. Therefore it relates to subjects. Students learn about subjects because these largely determine the curriculum; they are examined in these subjects even when their interests are cross-curricular. Andragogy accepts that interests can rarely be confined to traditional subject boundaries and considers learning needs to be more task- or problem-centred. The resultant learning is therefore directed towards a task or a problem, rather than a subject.

5 *Learning motivation* While it is expected in a pedagogical approach that students will be motivated towards the material, other factors such as the ability of tutors to raise students' commitment or make the material interesting, are also regarded as important. In the andragogical pattern the main source of involvement is the intrinsic interest of a student in what can be learned, and the opportunities this offers to raise self-esteem and self-confidence. These represent the chief motivators and provide the incentive for further learning.

From a tutor's perspective both negative and positive features emerge from such a contrast. First, many of them would argue that it is idealised. Few tutors would not welcome the chance (if only occasionally) to work with students capable of defining their learning needs, clear about their preferences, sure about their priorities and certain that their motivation is appropriately directed. Indeed that is the perfect situation towards which tutors strive, even in a didactic model, although its attainment could threaten their role.

However, most tutors would point out practical isssues which demand attention, and the extent to which these can flaw an andragogical approach, whatever its desirability. There are constraints imposed by resource scarcity, a syllabus, timetables, examination requirements, the expectations of students, and so on. Much of the time tutors perceive themselves driven to a pedagogic approach, when an adragogic stance could be far more suitable.

Second there are the positive characteristics of andragogy to be considered, and in particular the extent to which these might be linked to experiential learning practices. Undoubtedly these relationships become firmer the more mature the student group – indeed the notion of andragogy was first introduced in the context of adult learning – but they have significance whatever the learning capacity of the students. Children in secondary schools, for example, have developed considerable experience with learning cycles. In the context of what they want to know, they are well capable of achieving the most attractive features of andragogy, as they will have already demonstrated, possibly without either themselves or their tutors appreciating the opportunities offered.

Features of andragogy should point tutors towards appropriate behaviour for themselves and for their students. They can assist students to become more self-reliant, able to use previous experiences, aware of their readiness to learn and alert to what motivates them about a particular topic. The attitudes associated with adult learning do not have to be restricted to adults. They offer many potential benefits to experiential learning, irrespective of the different learning capacities of the students.

Student motivation

The most striking contrast that can be drawn between pedagogy and andragogy concerns student motivation. In pedagogic situations, the role of tutors is more obvious. Essentially it is their responsibility to ensure that students are motivated towards a topic. They organise the material, attempt to make the sessions interesting, and convince the students that it is in their best interests to learn. Tutors may blame the arrangements, the system or whatever, for a student lack of commitment, but they are unable to escape a corporate and professional duty to motivate their students.

Andragogically the place of tutors in motivating students is more oblique. Ideally, self-reliant students demonstrate maturity by defining their own needs and how these can best be satisfied. On this basis, tutors have a minimal role. However, they cannot abrogate responsibility for student motivation. It must remain the most important of all the aspects of student learning. Much of the time most students require some sort of motivating towards experiential learning, and often a tutor ought to be well placed to provide it.

An alternative way to describe the role of tutors is to say that they must encourage students about their capacity to behave andragogically, and demonstrate to students that it is in their interests to do so. Of course, this raises many practical problems in group situations. The notion of andragogy is dominated by the needs and perspectives of the individual student. The learning concept, previous experience, learning readiness and motivation represent unique features. Some students will be ready to learn, others will not. Some will be interested in a topic, others not, and so on.

A tutor can help students arrive at some sort of definition of their needs, but this is extremely difficult (if not impossible, with all but the smallest student group) to achieve on an individual basis. In some respects the problem of individuality promotes the notion of andragogy. Because of the shortage of time that a tutor can give to individual students, they have no option but to take responsibility for much of their own learning.

Of course this presents practical issues when students determine they have no need to learn. They may be unwilling to participate and remain passive, or they can try to inhibit or embarrass other students who appear to want to learn during a particular session. Sometimes students may attempt to divert a session towards other activities, either out of mischief or because they believe the new directions to be more appropriate to their own defininitions of need.

Tutors as motivators

Tutors have wide responsibilities for many facets of the learning environment – the topic, resources, previous student learning, timing and their own preferences. In the context of student motivation, other factors must be added, and these are a good deal less tangible. The topic planned can provide a stimulus to students' interests, but so can the attitude of a tutor towards that topic. If a sense of enthusiasm is conveyed, if the topic is introduced in an interesting and lively way, if the links with other topics are demonstrated, then students who were initially sceptical might well be attracted. For even in a state of andragogy few students have defined their learning needs in such a precise way that they know what they want or what they are going to reject. A topic may be of little immediate interest to a student, but because of the tutor's conviction and the manner in which the session is organised, many students can embark upon a valuable learning cycle.

With particular tutors some students will be highly motivated to learn, almost irrespective of the topic. They will have confidence in such tutors because they have helped them towards successful learning cycles. Perhaps they have made previous sessions enjoyable or they have helped students raise their self-esteem; almost certainly they will have persuaded students into clearer definitions of what they might want to learn and the most appropriate means of achieving these ends.

Such processes of support and encouragement ought to be the aim of tutors with all students. Their individuality (even with their imprecise definitions of needs) makes this aim unachievable. Not every student will have perceived the same success in previous sessions with a particular tutor; nor will each of them be stimulated in the same way or to similar extents by the tutor's enthusiasm and commitment to a topic.

Perhaps this variability among students is best illustrated by the issue of pace. A formidable task for every tutor is to pace a session appropriately. Andragogically, of course, this ought to be the responsibility of individual students, but the differences in their needs, interests and capacities mean that in a group context a tutor must strongly influence the speed at which a session progresses. Sometimes, therefore, a *Do* opportunity has to be curtailed even when some groups are still heavily involved, because other groups have apparently lost interest.

Occasionally a *Review* session has to be extended, when a few students have little left to add, because others remain engrossed in discussion. Often such situations can be used by an adept tutor to extend the learning of many students, including those who have apparently lost (or never had) interest. However there is always the likelihood that some students will fail (or refuse) to appreciate potential learning opportunities, even following tutor intervention; while others will perceive the same actions by the tutor to have been over-directive and feel that as a result their chances of gaining maximum benefit from a session have been blighted.

Choices made by tutors (particularly during a session) always risk demotivating some students, even when the intention is quite the reverse. Indeed so diverse are students' perceptions of their own needs in many groups, that some actions or suggestions by a tutor can simultaneously raise the interest of certain students towards a session, while lowering the interest of others.

The main risk of which tutors must be aware is not so much the single session that does not enthuse some (or all) of the students, for such situations will occur for every tutor, but that a series of sessions will have such an adverse impact on students that it reduces their enthusiasm for further learning. In effect, they decide that a particular tutor and membership of a certain group cannot motivate them, either because the topics appear irrelevant at this time, or the methods adopted do not appeal (or both). Such perceptions, even among a few students, are soon conveyed to others, particularly in groups lacking maturity where students are less able to define their own needs and judge whether the sessions are likely to satisfy them. Too often, perhaps, in such circumstances, tutors veer towards pedagogical assumptions about their students rather than attempting the more difficult and riskier approach of trying to help them develop a more andragogical perspective.

A supportive learning community

The advantages of a supportive learning community pervade all three intentions of a successful experiential learning session. First, it should assist students to gain something from the session itself by helping them establish at least one learning cycle relevant to the main activity. Second, a supportive environment ought to give students a chance to reflect upon and consolidate their attitudes about, and capacities towards, their own learning processes. Third, because of perceptions about success during the actual session, students should possess greater knowledge and skills for later sessions (and numerous other learning opportunities that might arise) and be better motivated towards them. Ideally, success makes them enthusiastic for more success, and a supportive learning community can promote appropriate attitudes.

However, tutors can pursue the notion of community too vigorously. They, themselves, are key members of the community. They must demonstrate by their interest, flexibility and participation that they are active members, not just to their own satisfaction, but also to the satisfaction of the students. In doing so, though, they may try to lead too forcibly, and this occurs most often when students are unable (or unwilling) to define their needs. Possibly they have had insufficient opportunity to consider what they want from a session. Alternatively they may have expectations but be unsure of whether a particular session is likely to realise them.

With all groups, but particularly the less mature, tutors are regularly faced with the problem that many students (and sometimes all) find it difficult to express their needs. Often in such circumstances tutors do not have the time to assist students make clear their particular requirements. Even when time is found, problems can still arise. Most usually these occur when students are helped to articulate their needs clearly but tutors feel unable to respond. Perhaps tutors are unprepared for the needs they reveal or feel that these needs do not match those that they wish to meet with this group (possibly on account of inadequate facilities) or are so diffuse as a group of needs that a single programme would be of little value.

If tutors do try to be affirmative in their leadership, then the chance exists that students will refuse the intended leads. They may be attracted intitially through the enthusiasm or the commitment of a tutor, but soon lose interest if the more long-term objectives appear not to be in line with their own definition of needs at the time. Sessions can sometimes appear to be extremely purposeful, but nevertheless overlook the main purpose of helping students formulate their own learning cycles. As in every activity, leadership is only effective if it induces those to whom it is directed to follow. Indeed the argument that all of the leadership must be provided by a tutor is difficult to reconcile with the notion of the learning community. In this context the more significant ideas that a tutor ought to seek relate to shared leadership and mutual support.

Shared leadership

Shared leadership does not imply no leadership by a tutor, which would mean an abrogation of responsibility. Rather, it involves a recognition that dependent upon circumstances, topic, previous experiences of students etc, certain leadership activities will be performed by students. On occasion perhaps a single student will lead a whole group; more frequently those will be interactions in smaller groups and a few students following examples set by others.

Sometimes such leadership is deliberately engineered (by any of the parties); at other times it happens by chance. In a similar way there can be a great deal of mutual support within a group, as students assist one another during the stages of a learning cycle. Perhaps one student explains a point to others, or uses a previous experience to illustrate a particular issue. Teams can be established during a *Do* activity, and the willingness of individuals to support one another in some circumstances can be discussed during the *Review* stage.

If the processes of shared leadership and mutual support become well developed in a group then there will be many examples of them occurring without the tutor being aware. Indeed should a tutor want to know, or try to find out every example, this would probably undermine the sharing and mutuality being sought. However, a tutor must continue to provide much of the leadership and considerable support (to small groups and individuals) particularly when the members are less mature.

In addition, a tutor has a prime responsibility for helping create the ambience within the group which permits shared leadership and mutual support to thrive. This has to be achieved simultaneously with assisting individual students gain the confidence that helps them acquire skills and knowledge. In effect, a tutor is trying to achieve a climate within a group where shared leadership and mutual support are endemic, so that all students (if possible) feel they belong and are advantaged by their membership. Individual learning within a group setting can then follow.

To achieve such a state of affairs, however, there must be frankness, openness and a respect for the capacities and the needs of others. Sometimes such facets of successful groupwork are unachievable because of the behaviour of a few students, or on account of how some students think others will react to what they might do or say. Tutors cannot inflict frankness, openness and common respect upon a group. Students cannot be instructed to respond to situations in ways conducive to an appropriate ambience. Indeed, instructions delivered by a tutor, or stern warnings, can often be counter-productive. All that tutors can do is lead their groups by example towards mutuality and sharing.

On occasion the leadership can be over-vigorous. This is especially the case when a tutor, through reputation or actions, is perceived by students as the main reason for lack of openness or honesty within the group. It can take a confident and competent tutor a long while to become aware of and accept such perceptions among students. Changing them presents still more problems, for of all behaviours in a group it is the tutors' which cause most interest to students.

Whether or not it regards itself as a supportive learning community, each group, provided it stays together for more than a few sessions, develops unique characteristics. It soon generates certain norms of behaviour. Strong personalities who try to move beyond those norms emerge. Relationships are formed which influence members' behaviour and also affect the attitudes of those who feel excluded. All of these developments are continuous. Norms are changed because of the actions of students or a tutor. New relationships are formed. Patterns of behaviour are dependent upon the topic or the way a tutor suggests the group should work.

There are few static elements in a learning community, yet most students have a need for continuity and some security. Tutors must first appreciate that their groups are functioning in a dynamic environment. A main part of their role is to provide balances – between their own leadership and that students contribute, and between stability and change. They can thus make a substantial contribution to the establishment of a supportive learning community.

Attitudes towards experiential learning

The nature of experiential learning makes it messy, which in turn makes it risky. Tutors are trying to assist students construct new and speedier learning cycles. There is always the chance that a *Do* stage may get out of hand. *Review* opportunities that were intended may not appear or, conversely, unexpected but valuable opportunities may emerge. Whether such outcomes result from mischief or good intentions on the part of the students is often irrelevant to potential critics of experiential learning.

Even when sessions progress more or less as planned it is easy for critics to find items upon which they can comment. A *Do* component might be dismissed as 'playing' by students, or a 'good game'. A *Review* element might be characterised as a meaningless discussion, perhaps dominated by one or two students only too keen (apparently) to voice their opinions on matters about which they know very little. If a tutor then goes on to assist students to conceptualise or generalise, a critic can wonder about any relationship between these activities and the *Do* and *Review* parts of the cycle, and indeed whether the session would not have been greatly improved if it had not started with some sort of tutor input. Finally, as the application of anything students might have learned cannot take place until after the session, and therefore is unobservable, a critic might well be satisfied that the whole exercise had been a waste of time.

Yet in all forms of teaching, whether narrowly didactic or wholly experiential, it is extremely difficult to measure the 'pay-off'. When a teacher organises a session there can be no certainty about what individual students will learn, nor even what that particular session might contribute to any learning which does occur. There is no clear technology of teaching or learning. Therefore anyone who chooses can be just as critical of a transmissive mode of teaching, and dismiss the resultant pupil experience as a complete waste of time. The subtle difference between didactic and experiential approaches is that when tutors choose to convey information or skills transmissively they ought to be able to minimise the messiness involved and as a result limit their risks. In effect they achieve these ends by professing to control the teaching-learning processes through making the students dependent upon them.

Not only is there a stronger control element in a didactic approach, its very existence increases the risks associated with experiential learning. In most secondary schools and colleges, transmissive styles have been dominant. The behaviour of tutors and students anticipated by these styles has become the norm. Attitudes have been moulded to what constitute conventional arrangements and therefore what is expected of a tutor and students during a session.

From a different viewpoint the resultant pedagogical stance builds up certain habits, and many tutors and students find these extremely difficult to break away from in order to formulate the new arrangements and different attitudes demanded by a more andragogical perspective. Achieving these transfers in behaviour, views and perceptions, at the same time as managing sessions, undoubtedly increases the risks involved with the organisation of experiential learning. The lack of a clear technology, whatever the approach, simply compounds the practical and attitudinal issues.

The attractions of 'playing safe', through sticking with a didactic approach, appeal to others as well as tutors. Students, or direct clients and their supporters (parents and employers), all want teaching and learning arrangements which they think will work. They have no wish to spend time on activities which do not appear to be meeting their needs (however difficult they find it to define them) or on activities which might meet their needs but are badly organised or prove impracticable. Therefore any experiential learning situations which prove unsatisfactory or seem to be purposeless can exaggerate the feeling that they are too risky. As a result, the pressure on a tutor, from students and others, to be successful with each and every experiential learning encounter is increased.

There is no more likely source for such increases in pressure than senior staff, and in particular college principals and headteachers. Perhaps they have had little opportunity to use experiential learning strategies in their own teaching, or possibly they have found themselves resolving problems created by disorganised or under-prepared sessions. Most likely though, any scepticism or doubt evolves from the nature of their own accountability. Ultimately they are responsible to governors, students, politicians and taxpayers for the work of the institution. It is a responsibility from which they are unable to escape. If there are criticisms of the work of the institution it is they who must answer. If the methods are judged to be inadequate it is they who will bear the brunt of the subsequent criticisms.

Transmissive styles of teaching and learning align more neatly with this particular model of accountability. The main task of tutors is to convey particular knowledge or certain skills to students. What these are can be described fairly easily in a syllabus or course content booklet. Whether the process of transfer has been successful, with which students, and to what extent, can also be checked without too much difficulty by some form of examination.

Indeed headteachers and principals can feel reassured that this accountability is visibly reinforced when the testing is done through third parties separate from the tutors. The success of the teaching can be checked in a manner which is seen (by outsiders) to be independent. Of course the checking becomes a more complex business when it tries to evaluate the level of learning achieved by each student, and issues like whether the material meets students' needs, the likely effects of the teaching and assessment processes, or student enthusiasm for further learning, receive minimal attention.

Promotion by good example

A real problem in trying to raise the status of experiential learning in the eyes of senior staff is that many of the claims that can be made in its favour are occasionally intangible and invariably immeasurable. It is difficult, for example, to quantify the enthusiasm of students in ways which a critic would find acceptable. A tutor might report that students have become much more responsive and believe that introducing elements of experiential learning into the sessions has been the main, if not the sole, contribution to such a change. It would be difficult, first, to demonstrate to an outsider any increase in responsiveness, and, second, to establish that a change in style has provided the most significant influence.

In the same way, tutors can sometimes find it difficult to convince senior colleagues that trying to help students define their own learning needs is anything more than a charade. These colleagues believe it to be a tutor's responsibility; or argue that in their experience tutors still organise their sessions in the same way, however students define their needs, and in any case there is no reliable way of assessing whether students have learned more because a session has started by trying to ascertain their own perceptions of needs.

Senior staff, and particularly headteachers and principals, obviously feel many responsibilities to their students, governors, parents and staff, for achieving value for money and being seen to run a well-organised institution. In such circumstances, there are many attractions in playing safe and limiting support for an experiential learning approach because of the messiness and risks associated with it. Often the attractions are increased by the expectations of outsiders. They anticipate that tutors will rely upon transmissive modes because that is the traditional and conventional way of doing things.

If didacticism is to be displaced from its position of eminence then the new arrangements will need to prove themselves better and more effective. Quantitatively this is impossible and therefore the need for tutors to elicit the support of senior staff for experiential learning becomes all the more significant. Pehaps the most appropriate way to do this is through involving them as fellow tutors. At the very least it has to be demonstrated to them first-hand that even with the messiness and the risks, experiential learning sessions are purposeful and involve processes to the benefit of students which are overlooked in transmissive styles of teaching.

By far the best way to establish greater emphasis on experiential learning is through good examples. Perhaps in the first place there are only a few tutors on the staff who act as proponents. They might involve others in such a way that the advantages of experiential learning permeate to a wider group. Students who have had successful and enjoyable experiences will usually accelerate this process, often inadvertently. Conversely, a few bad or disorganised experiences can produce much critical publicity.

As students and tutors become more confident and certain about the potential of experiential learning, opportunities open up to attract extra outside support. Indeed with changes elsewhere, on adult training courses, in management development activities etc, an increasing proportion of parents and governors are likely to have been involved in some organised experiential learning. There is no certainty, of course, that this will make them more favourable towards it. Nevertheless their awareness will have been raised, however effectively their tutors have exploited the potential of experiential learning. Indeed whatever the circumstances in which tutors use experiential learning, it is this process of exploitation which ought to be at the forefront of their thinking – how to achieve maximum benefit for the greatest number of students. The subsequent chapters consider the many practical issues which accompany the processes of exploitation.

PART 2

The Practice

5 Planning the programme

Selling the product

There was a time when any tutor using an experiential approach to learning was faced with the almost impossible task of convincing colleagues, and perhaps the headteacher or college principal, that what was to be attempted had academic validity and respectability. Experiential work out of doors, fieldwork and outdoor pursuits, for example, might have been acceptable, but within the more formal setting of the classroom or the lecture-room, things were different. The apparent lack of structure in many experiential learning activities, combined with the fact that students were not merely permitted but even encouraged to move around and to talk with one another, was frequently viewed with the gravest suspicion.

The situation is now likely to be somewhat different, and the development of experiential learning has been speeded by national initiatives such as the National Curriculum, TVEI and CPVE. All these emphasise, in one form or another, the importance of personal development, inter-personal skills and education in personal relationships (although this is not a core subject of the National Curriculum). It is precisely in such areas that experiential methods have shown themselves to be an ideal medium for learning and for the acquisition of self-knowledge and interpersonal skills.

Cynics and critics still remain, but the abundant evidence that now exists for the growth of maturity, self-reliance, self-knowledge and inter-personal and group skills brought about by experiential learning is persuasive. This, harnessed to the manifest enjoyment of what they are doing on the part of participants, means that while the journey is not yet complete, the up-hill part of it has largely been accomplished. However, there will still be institutions where much persuasion remains to be done, and tutors may find that this is best achieved by inviting colleagues to attend or assist with activities that are taking place, or, better still, by including experiential methods in the teaching staff's own development programme.

The total package

It has to be remembered that experiential learning is not an end in itself. It is simply one of a number of methods by which skills and knowledge can be increased. Any programme of learning requires variety if it is to be both effective and enjoyable. A mix of methods and approaches offers many potential advantages. It is therefore important to use experiential methods where they are most appropriate and best able to enhance the total programme. A programme or series of sessions based exclusively on experiential learning would be as inappropriate and lacking in variety as one solely employing didactic and transmissive styles of teaching.

If, for example, plans were being made for a school or college programme containing five major elements: 1 personal development; 2 career development; 3 survival skills; 4 health education; 5 civics.

1 The personal development module would find a major place for experiential learning by using materials and exercises designed to enhance maturity, self-reliance, cooperative and problem-solving skills, communication, giving and receiving of feed-back and so on.
2 Career development would contain a much stronger didactic element as students discovered information about job clusters and qualification requirements. There would be space for experiential activities aimed to help students develop such aspects as self-assessment skills and interviewing techniques.
3 Survivial skills would contain a mixture of styles – visits, talks and student-based research to discover about such things as mortgages, insurance and social security, with a more experiential approach to budgeting, bed-sit housekeeping and decision making in general.
4 Health education would probably have the least strong experiential element.
5 Civics would give scope for a combination of visits to law courts, council chambers and Parliament, with some transmissive teaching about the function of government and the institutions, and experiential work on decision-making in the local community and on ethical and moral considerations such as racial and sexual equality.

Similarly, in a course such as CPVE, the introduction of experiential learning at appropriate places is invaluable. This is most obvious in the module on Social Skills, where appropriate exercises are easily available to stress the importance of, and help students acquire, the skills needed for successful preparation and planning, communication, leadership, problem solving, negotiation, decision making, collecting, sharing and recording information, time-keeping and other relevant aspects of the topic. The same is true of other modules such as Personal and Career development.

Planning a module

The process of planning a module involving several sessions goes through five stages:

1 Establishing the aim of the module
2 Identifying and itemising the ground to be covered
3 Dividing the ground into sections
4 Allocating the material of the sections to individual sessions
5 Planning each session

If, for instance, a module is being planned on communication skills, the aim could be to ensure that course members became more effective in communicating with each other through all relevant modes. Tutors then need to list the themes it was hoped the module should cover. These would naturally include at some level the skills of listening, speaking, writing and reading and then, according to the nature of the total programme and the age, ability and stage of development of the students, such items as communication within a group or institution, interpretation of non-verbal communication, and the use of the media. The total material is then allocated between individual sections and the sections in their turn divided into sessions.

If the module was being planned for a CPVE group, the listening section could be divided into the following sessions:

1 Working in pairs, checking real hearing/listening
2 Prompting responses and disclosures
3 The importance of non-verbal communication
4 Types of misinterpretation and distortion and their dangers
5 Analysing argument and logic
6 The selection and recording of aural information
6 Coping with the telephone

The list is not exhaustive, of course, but it indicates the way in which sections can be sub-divided into sessions. There would also be further sessions in which the skills of listening were combined with other communicative skills to help students construct their own learning cycles and therefore raise their total competence in communication.

Planning a session

1 The group

While the principles for planning a session must always be based upon the four elements of the learning cycle – *Do, Review, Learn, Apply* – there are variables. These are largely influenced by the constitution of the group and the previous experiences of its members, both as individuals and as part of this particular group. The nature of the total programme will be important, also. Tutors will obviously be aware whether they have met the students involved before and/or whether they are going to meet them again or whether this is a one-off session. If the group situation is new, or if this is likely to be the only meeting, there will obviously not be time to build up anything other than a superficial relationship.

In such circumstances tutors have to be aware of the potential disadvantages either of introducing material in which there is a substantial risk factor (ie the potential for causing behavioural or emotional upset is high) or of leaving too many 'loose ends' at the completion of the session. If it is the group's first acquaintance with experiential learning in a formal setting, the nature of the exercise undertaken will normally need to be simpler than with an experienced group. While the material selected will vary according to the circumstances, it is essential that the tutor assesses the requirements of each group before any choice is made, rather than assuming that the same starting point can be taken on each occasion.

2 Observation skills

Because of the importance of *Review* in experiential learning it is often essential that the process of the exercise and the behaviour of the participants are observed carefully. An experienced group is likely to have developed the ability to observe its own process as the exercise proceeds, relying only on minimal help from a tutor. Groups in an earlier stage of development, or lacking in maturity will require observers. This can raise practical problems, particularly when the main group is sub-divided into smaller groups (perhaps even into pairs) for an activity. Unless there is a tutor to each smaller group (which is highly unlikely) or possibly between two such groups, these observers will have to be drawn from among the participants. Indeed, if circumstances and time permit, the tutor may wish to make the first activity with a new group an exercise to introduce students to observation so that all have at least the opportunity to develop the skills needed to undertake the role of observer.

The purpose of observers is to act as mirrors to the group, in order to reflect back to them what they have seen and heard taking place. As far as possible these processes ought to occur without any subjective comments or value judgements. A skilled observer may also enable members of a group to recall their own contributions, by asking the right questions, such as – *'What happened after . . . ?'* *'Who was it who said . . . ?'*

Good observation includes recording actual key phrases used by members of the group (far more effective than any reported speech), noting the timings of the activity and especially the actual times at which key events happened, and looking for non-verbal behaviour on the part of the participants. Only in this way will students be alerted to aspects of their actions, attitudes and behaviour which, because of their involvement in the activity, they are unable to record objectively for themselves. For example, a participant may deny taking any leadership role, while recorded speech shows comments like 'Leave that alone . . .' or 'Why don't we do it this way . . . ?'

If required, observers can record the quantity and type of verbal contribution made by each participant for a prescribed period during an exercise. It is possible to produce simple schedules to assist in these processes. Examples can be found in *Learning in Action* (Kirk, 1987) pp 29–37. With practice they are not difficult to use, although the ultimate effectiveness of observers depends on their ability to keep aloof from the actual proceedings and to make available to the group an accurate and impersonal record of what has been taking place. This can then be used by a group, and more especially individual students, to highlight various aspects of the *Review* stage and lead on to later stages of the learning cycle.

3 Choosing material

Each session will have an aim, for this will provide its purposefulness, and the exercise or activity chosen must be one which, in the view of a tutor, is likely to achieve this end. In addition, it is important that the learning process through which it is intended that the participants should pass is replicated in the exercises. For instance, the aim of a session may be that the students should learn the importance of knowing precisely what they are required to do before undertaking a task and the need to make the relevant enquiries if they do not have that knowledge. The exercise chosen must therefore be such that the outcome will be disastrous if the participants have not fully understood or listened to their briefing and if they have not had the good sense or confidence to ask for further information or clarification.

Care must be taken to ensure that the material is appropriate for the age, academic ability and cultural background of the students. Many exercises require a comprehension ability above that of less-academic school pupils. Some exercises from an industrial context are unattractive to those from non-industrial backgrounds, while others are decidedly male-orientated in their interest and presentation.

4 Preparation

It is crucial to the success of experiential learning that any exercise undertaken is professionally presented, fully prepared and runs with as few problems as possible. If tutors are using materials for the first time, or after considerable absence, they must ensure that they have mastered all the details, however irksome this may be. Instructions must be read carefully and, if necessary, briefing sheets prepared in the correct quantity. Any resources required need to be collected and sorted. If the exercise involves solving a logical problem, it may be as well for the tutors to have worked it out before the session. It is difficult to retain the confidence of the participants if they ask for an explanation of the solution of the problem and the tutor cannot provide it.

Timing needs to be checked, especially if there is any doubt whether the exercise chosen will fit into the time available. Thought must be given to the *Review*. Although this should contain a large measure of spontaneity, and certainly should not be rigidly constrained by the preconceptions of the tutors, they will want to have listed those learning points which they wish to see emerge. Finally, any follow-up materials need to be chosen and prepared, and any follow-up activities planned. The professional presentation of an exercise is an exact and sometimes time-consuming process and a far cry from the selection of another 'game' from the shelf to fill an otherwise empty slot in the programme.

The session

Presenting an exercise

Most experiential activities speak for themselves in that learning can take place at all stages – even those which are not identified in the guidance about the actual exercise. For instance, while it may be organisationally easier for a tutor to divide a class into sub-groups and allocate them places within the working area, there is potential for valuable learning if the participants are allowed to do this for themselves and reflect on it afterwards. It should not be necessary to do more than request them to form groups of a certain size.

In the same way, any good exercise will contain within its briefing all the information necessary for a group to function, and the tutor should refrain from adding to this information. Anything gratuitous by way of introduction, instruction or comment may simply deny the participants the opportunity for further learning, especially if they are likely to have difficulty in coping with the demands of the exercise as they are defined in it. The opportunity to *Review* the process by which they tackled any problems they met should not be hindered. During the course of the exercise, intervention should be avoided unless absolutely necessary. If, as is often the case, the groups are working against a time constraint, it is part of their task to make allowances for this and not one of the tutor's duties to remind them of it.

The Review

It is in the *Review* that the full learning from the activity should become apparent. This is, therefore, a most significant part of the session and adequate time must be allowed for it.

In the first minutes, groups will want to unwind and ventilate. In particular, if the exercise involved solving a problem or a competition between groups, they will want to know the solution and/or result and to have an opportunity within each group to make comment, serious or lighthearted.

When the *Review* proper commences, it is probably wise to start by inviting groups to comment on their performance, to assess whether they achieved their target, and to describe the processes through which they have passed. They will be helped in this by the observers who will be able to give objective insights to correct the group's own (probably) subjective comments. They will then be in a position to discuss, in the light of this evidence, whether they could or should have tackled the problem differently or better.

In addition to any particular learning points which a tutor may wish to highlight, a number of items are likely to come up on a recurrent basis. These usually include:

- the structure of the group and the arrangements of the working idea;
- leadership of the group and roles within it;
- the contribution (constructive or destructive) of individual members;
- communication, together with the methods used for collecting, collating, recording and sharing information;
- time-keeping;
- the means used to reach any decisions which were taken;
- any other relevant inter-personal behaviour.

Tutors, however, should try to avoid cramming the *Review* into a strait-jacket and ought to allow learning points which are of concern to any group or individual to emerge. Given sensitivity and listening skills on the part of the tutor and an appropriate degree of receptivity and informality within the working environment, this should occur quite naturally.

Follow-up and the application of the learning

At the close of the *Review* stage, a tutor should have allowed sufficient time to discuss with students the relevance and applicability of what they have learned and to provide them with any follow-up materials or further guidance necessary. For instance, a group may have undertaken the task of selling an object to a prospective purchaser, and the *Review* may have opened up discussion about the strategy and tactics of the 'salesperson', the skills needed to persuade a wary or reluctant 'customer', and the morals and ethics of 'selling' in general.

A tutor might want to ensure that as far as possible students have realised for themselves the relevance of this learning to their own potential role as 'salesperson'. Perhaps the students are a group of teaching or lecturing staff and for them the key issue could be the selling of the school or college to potential students and their parents or employers. For other students an equivalent relevance might be their thinking about the whole process of 'selling' themselves during job interviews or for a place in college. Teaching may be required to support what has emerged in discussion, and handouts or videos about good and bad presentation skills may also be helpful. Clearly, a tutor will need to have thought through in advance any materials which may be called upon during the follow-up stage.

Some potential practical problems

However well-prepared tutors may be, situations arise which can place them in difficult or trying circumstances. They arise because of the nature of experiential learning, and the likelihood of unexpected personal interactions associated with it. Such situations are unpredictable and a factor in inhibiting less experienced tutors from introducing and exploiting experiential learning opportunities. Because such situations cannot be anticipated, it is clearly impossible to be precise about when they will occur, but six broad areas which can create practical problems for tutors are described below. In each a number of strategies are suggested which have proved successful in assisting the learning processes.

1 Dealing with silence

One of the most disconcerting moments for all tutors, but in particular for those lacking in experience, is when a group, for whatever cause, falls silent at a time when its participation could normally be expected. If an individual student is involved the situation is less acute as, if necessary, a tutor can elicit any doubts or difficulties which have induced an individual to remain silent on a one-to-one basis. But when the entire group falls silent, a tutor may feel threatened with the collapse of a whole teaching session.

There is no standard advice which can be given for handling the situation as it can come about for so many different reasons. These include a distaste for the activity in which the group is involved; boredom with the exercise; a lack of rapport with a tutor; external distraction; or insecurity and fear of appearing foolish by taking any initiative. Under the circumstances, it is unwise for a tutor to break the silence too soon. After all, the activity may be more complex for the participants than a tutor realises and they may need time to plan their response.

If an intervention is made, it is more likely to be productive if it tackles the problem of the silence rather than suggesting a change of activity. 'I am puzzled by your silence at this point' is likely to produce some response and ease the log-jam. For instance, if the group or members of it claim that they find the exercise boring or childish the tutor can then move directly into the *Review* stage and initiate a discussion on the process by which this fact emerged. Why was it, for instance, that the group fell silent rather than tell the tutor of its dissatisfaction? How would participants handle a similar situation in the future? A discussion on these lines may well not only prevent further silences of this nature, but may also lead to greater understanding between members of the group and between the group and the tutor.

2 Timing and intervention

For an inexperienced tutor, one of the greatest temptations is to try to do too much in a single session. Possibly because of a natural fear of running out of material before the session is ended, there is a tendency to include too many activities or to concentrate to such an extent on the exercise that there is insufficient time for the *Review* or follow-up arrangements. With older groups in particular, the amount of discussion which is likely to be aroused by a well-written and presented exercise means that a substantial amount of time is needed to give a chance for all the learning in the *Review* to emerge.

It is unlikely that less than half an hour will be sufficient for most *Reviews*; in longer working sessions more may be needed. Time has also to be allowed for any efforts by tutors to help their students towards generalisations and conceptualisations. Often time is also needed to discuss how some aspects of the learning may be applied away from the classroom or lecture-room. This means that in many two-hour sessions the actual experiential activity may last for as little as 30 minutes. Of course there are circumstances (particularly with more mature groups) when the *Do* stage has already occurred because of the relevant previous experiences of group members.

Another difficulty for the inexperienced tutor is to gauge the most appropriate moment at which to intervene (if at all). Again, through fear of the situation getting out of the tutor's control, the temptation is to act too soon and thereby to destroy opportunities for learning. Often in the *Review* the group can gain enormous insights about group processes and interpersonal relationships if (during the activity) their plans have gone totally awry, if the group has fallen apart, if they were confronted with a problem which they could see no way to resolve, or if serious clashes of personality have occurred. Such happenings are, after all, genuinely 'experiential' and replicate just those situations which students will be familiar with in everyday life. By giving help to a group in difficulty too soon or by hastening to resolve conflict within a group, a tutor may deprive the participants of the opportunity of handling these situations for themselves.

If a tutor does feel it necessary to intervene, this can be done least destructively by using techniques similar to those described in dealing with silence; in other words by asking questions which help the group's members to make progress for themselves. 'At what stage do you feel your plans started to go wrong?' 'If you go back to that stage, are there other ways in which you could tackle the problem?' More generally, intervention should be used as late and sparingly as possible and only when stalemate has been reached or on those occasions when participants need rescuing from situations in which they may suffer emotional damage.

3 The challenge to the tutor

There will be situations when a tutor feels challenged by a group or by one or more individual members. These may happen for a variety of reasons and in a number of different ways. Some individuals may simply be so extrovert or insensitive to the needs of other group members that they cannot be restrained from dominating the entire activity. Or someone may be intent on disrupting the group's working for a personal reason. It may be a natural or contrived eccentric whose actions become a nuisance, a distraction or a threat to the tutor or to the rest of the group. On one occasion, for example, a male member of a newly-formed group, whose members did not know each other, produced his knitting – which engaged his attention throughout the length of the activity!

These kinds of individual challenge can normally be left until the *Review* where the total group is likely to talk them through and sort them out – except for the knitter who posed such a threat to his colleagues that none of them had apparently noticed him at all! Failing that, an objective comment by a tutor, uttered in an unemotional way, can often lead to a solution of the problem: 'I find it difficult to conduct the session as I had planned because you are playing such a dominant role' 'You make me feel that the exercise isn't satisfying your needs when you knit throughout the activity'. In comments of this kind it is essential to keep the delivery low-key and to avoid appearing to be defensive.

A more direct challenge, either from an individual or a group, can occur when there is frustration and possibly anger as a result of failure or emotional trauma. A group which has performed incompetently in an exercise or which has been overshadowed by another group may blame the tutor and demand to know why they have been made to waste their time in such a childish activity. On one occasion an individual who, in the course of a negotiation exercise, had broken the undertaking he had given in a totally uncharacteristic way, projected his action onto the tutor with the words 'You made me cheat'. In cases such as this, a tactic which is normally successful is to return the question to the plaintiff 'What makes you feel the activity is childish?' 'How was it that I made you cheat?' In answering such questions, dialogue is normally resumed and the process of the exercise can be examined as in a normal *Review*. Once again, however, it is essential for a tutor to have the confidence and the competence to remain calm and to keep the exchanges unemotional.

4 Testing boundaries

One important facet of experiential learning, which can easily be overlooked, is that of testing boundaries. Traditional upbringing in childhood, followed by conventional schooling, incubates in many people the behaviour pattern of abiding by the rules and waiting for directions. Experiential learning provides an excellent opportunity to back away from this culture, not in the sense of attempting to produce rebels, but by encouraging students to be responsible for their own behaviour, to take initiatives without waiting to be told, and to undertake imaginative and possibly risky ways of solving problems unless or until specifically prohibited from doing so.

With younger or less-mature students, this process may include gaining the confidence to move furniture or rooms without seeking permission, to demand further information about resources for an exercise without waiting to be given them, or to decide that not all members of their group are needed for a given activity (it might even be better undertaken without them all) and so to release some to undertake something else or to relax with a cup of coffee. Older students may still be as inhibited as younger ones and may need to learn to test boundaries in simple areas such as those described above. In addition, they may challenge the structure and rules of the exercises and even withdraw from an activity altogether. Clearly, such situations can provide immense practical problems, but provided all students are present at the *Review*, and prepared to discuss the process of what has been going on, the learning available can be substantial.

5 Competitiveness

Given that competitiveness is a basic drive for a great many human beings, experiential learning is an ideal medium for gaining understanding of how it can become either a positive or negative force. Activities can be planned which cover one or all of these aspects of competitiveness.

a) Competitiveness as a positive force
A group which has been set a task to complete, or a problem to solve, as speedily and effectively as possible, has to be competitive. There need be nothing aggressive or destructive about this. If our aim is to encourage students to develop efficient methods of group work and to learn to solve problems with maximum speed and competence, one test of their having achieved this is their ability to reach correct conclusions faster than others. There is nothing to be ashamed of in wishing to be the best. *Invisible Load* and *Darlington Station* (two exercises described more fully in Chapter 11) are admirable examples of ways in which the positive facets of competitiveness can be considered.

b) Competitiveness as a negative force
There are many occasions on which, because two groups are traditionally rivals (eg neighbouring schools or colleges) or have been nurtured in an atmosphere of mutual suspicion (eg traditional management and unions), they are unable to work together when it is in both their interests to do so. Exercises are available, especially in the field of negotiation, where because both parties set off with a 'win/lose' mentality, they end up in a 'lose/lose' situation when a 'win/win' one was available. From this, participants can easily see the danger of competitiveness in its negative form.

Two good examples of this type of exercise are included in the Exercise Section. Both were derived by Tony Brennan from an old and well-known activity, probably best known as *Prisoner's Dilemma*. The first of these is *Push-Pull*. The nature of the competition is largely determined by the objective of the exercise as presented to students once the main group has been divided into two teams. It can be offered in an entirely non-judgemental way: 'The objective of this exercise is for your group to end up with a positive score'. The neutrality of the tutor can be enhanced by allowing the group to divide itself into two teams, using criteria it has agreed. However, it is difficult for a tutor to establish complete neutrality, according to the perceptions of all students, because of the role (which could of course be delegated to a student) of revealing the colour played by the teams in each round and the subsequent announcement of scores. Only the tutor, or delegated student, is privy to the round by round declarations of each group.

The nature of the competition can be changed effectively by altering the original objective; for example, 'The objective of the exercise is to beat the other team'. Competitiveness can be further heightened by the possibility of monetary rewards or losses; 'The objective of the exercise is for you to make (or lose) money for your group'. If the stakes are large enough, tutors can find themselves bribed to declare 'false' results – when only they know the actual declarations of both teams in every round. A system of rewards and payments is included with the exercise. With such nuances the *Do* and *Review* sections can become lively and interesting. Most students stand to learn a good deal about competition, the difficulties in maintaining 'win/win' situations, the superficial attractions of 'win/lose' situations (if you are the winner) and the incipient risks of 'lose/lose' situations.

A more complex variety of the exercise (*Sum*) involves dividing the main group into three teams – Red, Blue and Green. Each team has two numbers which add to seven (1 and 6, 2 and 5, 3 and 4) – hence the title Sum. Each team must use one number per round. The team score for each round is determined by the aggregate total of the three numbers. The learning opportunities are greater than in Push – Pull but their achievement is more demanding on the tutor.

The same variations in the exercise are possible. The objective of the exercise can be presented neutrally – 'to score positively' – or with varying degrees of competitiveness – 'to beat the other two teams'. Alternatively, competitiveness can be sought by offering a financial gain (or loss) element. On this occasion, though, the competition is three-sided and the difficulties of maintaining a 'win/win' situation greatly enhanced. Negotiation both between groups and among group members can become convoluted. Two teams may attempt to exclude the third team. Individuals are likely to view the competition in different ways. For a skilled tutor numerous learning opportunities become available.

c) 'Cheating' or using the invented wheel?
It can easily happen that when two or more groups are working in the

same room, even if there has been no suggestion that the task on which they are both engaged is competitive, a basic competitive instinct takes over and they start to compete automatically. Planning time for the exercise may have been allowed, but as soon as one group starts on the task the others follow for fear of being left behind. One group may try to see what another is doing and be accused of 'cheating'.

During the *Review* a tutor should be able to highlight the fact that as no competition was involved the 'cheaters' were acting entirely sensibly. The comparison could be two similar educational establishments engaged on setting up similar courses. What could be more sensible than for the one which was later into the field to ask the other for advice as to its experience in the early stages and thus avoid reinventing the wheel? And, sadly, how often this kind of cooperation fails to take place because of some imagined competitiveness or suspicion.

6 Giving and receiving feedback

Giving and receiving feedback can pose problems for many, if not the majority, of both tutors and students. When commenting on the performance of a colleague, for example, tutors tend to avoid saying too much that is critical for fear of giving offence, especially if they think they are referring to problems caused by someone's personality rather than by particular actions. They may also be nervous about potential comment on their own performance if discussion becomes too frank. Again, some tutors are often inhibited in commenting on a student's personality or behaviour in a positive way in case it causes embarrassment.

In the same way when students are giving feedback to their peers after an exercise there is a tendency to be aggrieved or at least defensive if the comments appear critical, and self-deprecatory if they are complimentary. If a student is praised for something done well, a false modesty can follow, characterised by the claim that 'It was really nothing' or that 'Anyone could have done it'.

The openness, honesty and objectivity in *Review*, which are necessary to produce the maximum learning from any experiential activity, will never be achieved as long as this combination of inhibition, embarrassment and defensiveness is around. To help overcome this, exercises which have been devised to help students develop increased skill in giving and receiving feedback are particularly important. The hope is that eventually a typical response to a critical comment will be, 'I'm interested that you found my contribution to the group destructive. Please tell me more about this'. And to a piece of complimentary feedback, 'I'm glad you found my presentation helpful. I had taken a lot of trouble preparing it, and I'm pleased it went so well'.

6 Selecting, using and producing materials

What to look for

With practice and experience (their own experiential learning) tutors can overcome many of the potential problems discussed in the previous chapter. However, the speed with which they gain confidence will be closely related to the availability of good materials on which to base student experiences. A variety of materials for experiential learning is available, and many of these are suitable for adaptation or alteration to accommodate the needs of individual tutors.

When starting to use an experiential mode, however, it is important that tutors are clear about what they are looking for in any of the materials they use. Some of those available are not really designed for experiential learning as defined in this book. Many, for example, aim to increase self-analysis and raise self-awareness through the completion and discussion of questionnaires and other instruments. Surprisingly little experiential learning activity is generated even during discussion, largely because individual students are rarely keen to join a public *Review* of a private activity – completing a self-assessment questionnaire. It is also noticeable that students tire quickly of this kind of activity, particularly if it is introduced on a regular basis.

Other materials aim to achieve learning through role-play, but this again, while it may contain the possibility of experiential learning, can often be rather disappointing in its outcomes. A main disadvantage is that participants can become over-involved in the acting element. As a result they do not necessarily go through an experience which enables them to review their own natural (sometimes subconsciously driven) behaviour, particularly as observed by others. The role takes over and the whole activity becomes artificial (see Chapter 11). While both self-analysis questionnaires and role-play can contribute to experiential learning (and have legitimate functions in their own right) they are unlikely to be very productive, and for this purpose they receive no further attention here.

Commercial packages

Tutors searching out good-quality materials can find some among those designed specifically for use in schools, colleges and other educational establishments. There is also a vast quantity of material produced mainly to promote management development. Here the target audience includes organisations (of many types and sizes), individuals looking towards self-development and course designers who are always searching for new material to ensure that their training activities appear new, interesting and in line with the needs of their students.

Over the last 15 years a number of aids to experiential learning have appeared on educational book lists. The earliest of these emerged from backgrounds other than the specifically experiential. Materials were designed to foster Personal and Social Development courses, of which the most notable was the *Active Tutorial* programme. While mainly employing pen and paper, questionnaire and discussion methods, they also offered the opportunities for experiential learning.

Other materials were designed for the teaching of Drama, by such pioneers as Dorothy Heathcote and Donna Brandes. These exercises aimed to build confidence, trust, self-knowledge and teamwork and were essentially experiential, although the range of learning aims they covered was limited.

The earliest specifically experiential materials used in schools and colleges were borrowed and adapted from the world of industry and commerce, and were fostered by firms with outstanding training records such as ICI and Marks and Spencer. In parallel, pioneers such as John Adair, the Tavistock Institute and the Coverdale Organisation also developed and used materials of this kind. An extensive range of activities designed and developed in North America had also been available for some time. Although expensive to obtain, some of these, when adapted for a specific group, prove very useful. An annotated list of materials from such sources most suitable for use in educational establishments appears at the end of the chapter.

New tutors, in particular, are often concerned about the 'source' of an exercise. Perhaps they think that material specifically produced for use in educational institutions is inherently more appropriate for their students than that written for an industrial context. Occasionally there is a gulf. Material exists which quite clearly has been designed to meet the training needs of particular industries. In the main it would be unsuitable for use with school or college students. However, the key word is 'appropriate'. Ultimately, of course, it is the students who determine whether an exercise satisfies their needs, but an important role of a tutor is to offer material which ought to meet the needs of most students, irrespective of its origins.

For tutors, therefore, the main issue is whether material is appropriate, given the type of group, its previous experiences, the learning environment and the expectations of individual students. *The Indivisible Load* for example (see page 176) although originally written for middle managers at ICI, has been used successfully with fourth and fifth year groups in schools. It has also been used to great effect in the management training of senior staff to acquaint them with some aspects of communication skills, and as an aid to team building; while an exercise like *Orange Market* (*Learning in Action*, pp 117–118), designed to assist pupils prepare for job interviews, has proved suitable for headteachers thinking about how to 'sell' their schools in the competitive environment of the Education Reform Act and Local Management of Schools.

Designing your own material

Many tutors, as they become attracted to experiential learning, think that the most effective route towards appropriate exercises is to write their own, and so design their own materials. The advantages of this route are obvious. Exercises can be specifically tailored to a particular course or module. The appropriate academic and intellectual level can be established and a framework and setting chosen which is suitable for and congenial to the student client group. Also, tutors who know their groups well are best placed to consider what details ought to be included to satisfy student needs. The only drawback is, of course, that devising and writing exercises is time consuming.

Chapter 7 looks in detail at what is involved in tutors producing their own materials by considering, step-by-step, the development of an exercise. The starting point was a realisation by a tutor of the need for new material to assist students increase their self-awareness. Throughout the periods of design and trialling a diary was kept. Significantly, as the development of the activity continued so did the possibility that it could be used with other student groups and to achieve different objectives. Those stages in the evolution of the exercise are also described.

By contrast, but in a similar manner, Chapter 8 examines how an existing published exercise can be adapted for a number of alternative uses. Here the characteristics of a good exercise are studied, alongside the modifications tutors might wish to make to ensure that published materials accord with the objectives they and their students wish to accomplish. Sometimes these can be quite different from those that the designers assign to their exercises.

Converting non-experiential situations into experiential ones

With many classes it is possible for tutors to integrate didactic and experiential approaches. For some topics it may appear more sensible to a tutor to adopt a didactic format; for other topics and different circumstances the experiential model may be better suited. Criteria that might be used to judge which approach (or which combination of approaches) is most suitable are suggested in Chapter 5. However, because of the traditions and expectations associated with transmissive modes of teaching, and the unfamiliarity of many tutors with experiential learning situations, many tutors persist with a didactic style when their students would appreciate the additional opportunities to control their own learning that can be presented by experiential learning.

Three examples (drawn from student groups of varying maturities) reinforce the point admirably.

1 As part of a communications module in a one-year 6th form course, it had been customary to include sessions on using the telephone. These involved discussing and devising telephone message pads, identifying the skills and techniques required to use them effectively, and undertaking a number of written exercises. These included describing responses that the student would make to certain types of call and taking messages to pass on to colleagues.

   The advent of Work Experience led to comments from employers that, despite the work which has just been described, students still seemed apprehensive of and incompetent in using the telephone for business purposes. It was decided, therefore, to introduce an experiential element into the learning. Students were asked to write down the functions they had performed on Work Experience, the type of telephone calls they or their colleagues might expect in this work, and the information they would need to answer queries or deal with complaints. Time was allowed to prepare and collect any equipment or resources that were necessary, and then, using the school's internal telephone system, 'real' calls were made. These were observed and monitored by other students and the tutor and were then discussed in *Review*. Finally an opportunity was arranged for individuals to take charge of the school telephone exchange and operate it with the support and guidance of the office staff.

2 With more mature groups, such as teachers trying to improve their understanding of, and skills in, for example, management, exercises are needed which build upon their previous experiences, and also allow (as far as possible) a common experience. If the issues being considered include leadership styles and how staff perceive they are being managed (whatever their seniority) there are many advantages in

starting with a practical activity. Students can be offered scenarios and two are included in the Exercise Section (p 194). In both cases students must make a judgement about how they would respond to a particular situation which has arisen when a teacher requests time out of school. Students can be asked to write down their own responses, which can then be compared to those of other students, both in smaller groups and in the main group. During the *Review* and as a follow-up, a tutor can then expand points as they emerge – about the head-to-teacher relationship, the effects of whatever is decided on staff motivation, the problems of establishing procedures etc. They can offer a number of theoretical insights (where appropriate) and possibly attempt some generalisations about leadership, motivation or other management issues.

With some slight rewording the exercise can also be used with non-teachers; it elucidates discussion on management styles and interpersonal actions, whatever the type of organisation. Also, substituting Jim Smith for Jane Smith, and Madge Scrivens for Geoff Scrivens in the material handed to students, means that a number of gender issues can be considered.

3 When teachers are the students, staff development matters are often best introduced through experiential means. Students can be asked to devise a development programme for Jeremy Isis and development targets for Jane Ryder (full details on pages 192 and 193 in the Exercise Section). Again, the most appropriate approach is to ask individual students to make their own written reponses before moving to a group discussion situation. These responses vary considerably, often depending upon the seniority and previous experiences of the students. Such points can be drawn out by a tutor during the *Review*, and significant staff development issues introduced by a tutor in the light of these two particular examples.

The point being made is not that experiential is necessarily better or more appropriate than non-experiential. These examples try to show, however, ways in which an apparently non-experiential situation can be converted into experiential activities. It is for tutors, assisted by their students on many occasions, to assess the suitability of a particular approach. The key issue in this context is that, for reasons discussed in earlier chapters, tutors often continue with a non-experiential prog-ramme because they are not aware of how they might exploit any experiential opportunities or do not have the confidence to do so.

Evaluation of material

After any exercise has been used, it is important that a tutor finds time to evaluate its success. Such evaluation is, of course, crucial on the first occasion on which particular material is tried. If time permits, it is valuable every time an exercise is used subsequently as outcomes can vary surprisingly depending on the client group, the physical circumstances in which the exercise is undertaken, and the purpose for which it has been employed. It would be remiss to assume that because an exercise has been a relative success or failure on its first use, this will always be the case.

The success or failure of an exercise can be judged in a number of ways. Some of these, though apparently trivial, can be important. For instance, Did the students enjoy the exercise? Was it pitched at the right intellectual level? Did it sit comfortably within the time allowed for it? Were the logistics of it easy to handle or was it too demanding either in the preparation or resources required for it?

None of these factors, however, is remotely as important as whether the *Review* gave evidence that the learning which the tutors intended had in fact resulted from the exercise. If such learning does not occur, an exercise cannot be said to have been successful.

Without a *Review* and follow-up an activity cannot be regarded as an opportunity for experiential learning as defined. In such circumstances an activity is no more than an opportunity for a 'good game' or a fill-in. If exercises are used in this manner, students' enthusiasm for experiential learning will soon be blunted. However, other learning can emerge which shows an exercise to be valuable for purposes which have not been mentioned in any list of published objectives, and indeed had not been envisaged by those designing the exercise. In the experience of the authors, in nearly every case in which they have used exercises they have found learning emerging in addition to, or different from, that expected, and in ways which had not occurred when an exercise had been used with another student group. This confirms the capacity of students to construct their own learning cycles.

It is also wise to remember that the outcome of an exercise is likely to vary, at least partially, every time it is used. Nothing is to be gained, therefore, from rejecting an exercise out of hand on the grounds that a colleague has been unsuccessful with it or that its nature, language or setting is unfamiliar or unattractive to oneself.

The authors had the amusing experience of having an exercise rejected by one publisher on the grounds that it had not been appropriate for the purpose for which it was designed and, moreover, that the setting of the exercise, a school's promotion committee, was too unrealistic to be taken seriously. In fact the exercise had been based exactly on the system in use in an existing school. It has now been published (Kirk 1987, pp 154–159) and used with considerable success in several contexts, by staff in schools to assist them learn about issues related to promotion, and with students from quite different backgrounds. In the latter case factors relating to working in groups, establishing and agreeing criteria among individuals, and sharing of information can be used to enhance individual learning cycles. It is always unwise to come to conclusions about the effectiveness of an exercise on the basis of one use with one particular group.

Good experiential learning

The single most important criterion which determines the quality of an exercise is whether it works, that is, whether it enables students to build a learning cycle. However, that is far too glib a response. As discussed in the previous section, an exercise may work in one context – according to a tutor – but not in another, though the tutor may have thought the two situations were not too dissimilar in terms of physical conditions, timing and student grouping. Such a comparison, however, still overlooks the issue of what is implied by an exercise 'working'. In this example an observer could have judged that on neither occasion did experiential learning occur.

Once again it is the individuality of the learning achieved by each student which must dominate any judgements. An exercise has produced successful experiential learning if it assists most (but not necessarily all) students to go through the various stages of a learning cycle, the objectives of which align with those expected by, or judged valuable to, tutor and students.

In many ways a single checklist like the one below can be misleading, because not every item need be relevant to a particular session of experiential learning. It also implies that a judgement is possible (and ought to be made) about each item. Nevertheless, with these caveats, tutors may find it useful to discuss informally – with colleagues, and where possible students – the following features which help in assessing the quality of experiential learning achieved with one student group through using a particular exercise.

Checklist

1 Does the *Do* session involve all students?
2 Are there some occasions when some students have no wish to be involved in the exercise, particularly if they have usually participated in activities of this type?
3 Is the involvement of students active and committed, rather than 'going through the motions' because that is what the tutor expects?
4 Are the instructions clear?
5 Is *Review* a natural procedure following the *Do* stage?
6 Has the tutor to stimulate discussion or is this largely achieved through the qualities of the exercise?

7 Can most students, irrespective of their roles in the exercise, contribute to the *Review*?
8 Has the *Do* stage provided experiences which can be compared with experiences gained elsewhere?
9 What opportunities emerge from the *Do* and *Review* stages for a tutor to help students conceptualise from their experiences?
10 Do most students (if not all) have the opportunity to proceed through the four levels of learning in a particular topic as a result of the exercise?
11 Are the application and transfer of knowledge (the later learning levels) which can result from the exercise alignable with the skills and knowledge which students seek?
12 Are students normally satisfied with the whole exercise and related activities?

More specific items relating to the *Do* and *Review* stages of experiential activities are considered in Chapter 10. Such a checklist offers tutors guidance in selecting, using and adapting published materials, and some assistance in the production of their own material.

Sources of experiential learning material

Adair, J. and Despres, D. (eds) (1978 and 1980) *A Handbook of Management Training Exercises – Vols 1 and 2*. British Association for Industrial and Commercial Education.
A collection of over 50 exercises which are carefully explained. Although intended for supervisors and managers in industry many are suitable for schools/colleges after some minor modifications. Some, however, require considerable resources.

Brandes, D. and Phillips, H. (1980) *The Gamesters' Handbook: 140 games for teachers and group leaders*. Hutchinson Education.
This book provides a large collection of exercises, many of which are suitable for use or adaptation.

Forbess-Green, S. (1983) *The Encyclopaedia of Ice Breakers*. Applied Skills Press, San Diego.
A valuable source book of structure activities that are said to 'warm-up, motivate, challenge, acquaint and energise'.

Kirk, R.F. (1987) *Learning in Action*. Basil Blackwell.
30 useful exercises are included, as mentioned in the introduction.

Morris, K.T. and Cinnamon, K.M. (1983) *A Handbook of Verbal (and non-verbal) Group Exercises*. University Associates.

Although 'Californian' in style, these two books contain the odd idea for designing a suitable exercise.

Pfeiffer, J.W. and Jones, J.E. (eds) *Annuals (72–85) For Facilitators, Trainers and Consultants*. University Associates.
In addition to the annuals, there is also a collection of Handbooks. Together they form an excellent source of materials and ideas; indeed many exercises found elsewhere seem to derive from this source.

Simon, S.B., Hawe, L.W. and Kircshenbaum, H. (1978) *Values Clarification*. Hart.
Primarily concerned with values clarification, this book contains a wealth of material which can be used experientially in many different contexts.

Steeh, E. and Ratcliffe, S.A. (1976) *Working in groups – a communication manual for leaders and participants in task-oriented groups*. National Textbook Company, Illinois.
This book is intended for use by small groups that must accomplish tasks or work within specified periods of time.

Thayer, L. (ed) (1981) *50 Strategies for experiential learning – Books 1 and 2*. University Associates.
This book contains some useful ideas for experiential activities.

Woodcock, M. (1979) *Team Development Manual*. Gower.
Woodcock, M. and Francis, D. (1981) *Organisation and Development through team building*. Gower.
A series of analytical approaches to the investigation of the working situations students or groups of students might find.

7 Writing an exercise

'Reality' – an exercise in self-awareness

To demonstrate the process of writing an exercise (as described in the previous chapter) a 'diary' was kept of the production of an exercise designed to increase the self-awareness of the participants. This recorded the development as it occurred. The need for such an exercise had been confirmed for the tutor by his experiences with two different groups of clients: pupils and teachers. In the course of discussion on career possibilities with pupils, it had become apparent that many of them had an unrealistic concept of their own skills, aptitudes and capabilities and seriously considered themselves as candidates for jobs for which they were quite unsuited. In a similar way, teachers viewed themselves as candidates for promotion but had neither the qualifications nor the experiences appropriate to the particular post which interested them; often they did not realise that such qualifications and experiences would be required. The nature and context of 'Reality', therefore, would make the exercise appropriate for use with either group of clients.

Aim and process

The aim of *Reality* was that participants should realise that there is an inevitable match between jobs and the skills and qualifications which go with them. What, then, was the learning process through which particpants were to go in order to reach this conclusion? There were a number of points which it was hoped that the exercise would cover:

1 That thought must be given to the requirements of any post before it is assumed that one is a suitable candidate for it.
2 That there is a skill in matching one's capabilities, qualifications and experience to relevant jobs.
3 That all participants will become aware that there are some posts for which each of them will never be realistic applicants and that there is no shame in that.

4 That when missing qualifications and experiences have been identified, some of these can be learnt or acquired.

Such a learning process would demand that the context of the exercise
itself would contain as many as possible of the following elements:

1 A temptation to jump at the 'job' because superficially it appeared
simple.
2 The possibility of finding that one's 'talents' were not appropriate for
the 'job'.
3 The opportunity of taking remedial action by:
a) honing one's existing talents;
b) acquiring new skills;
c) employing outside help;
d) looking for a different job.
4 The opportunity to observe that within any given group of people
there is a likelihood that one or more will be able to do the 'job' easily,
some will be able to acquire the skills necessary for it, but some will
always find it beyond them.

Finding a suitable medium

Given the specifications above, the next stage was to devise an exercise
which would incorporate as many of these as possible. A number of ideas
were considered in different areas.

The first idea looked at was to use something mechanical such as
some kind of lock or catch. This could appear very easy to undo at first
sight, but in fact be far more complex than first appearances might
suggest. Participants would have to learn the skills to undo it either by
using problem-solving techniques or by seeking advice. An alternative in
the same field could be a building exercise, comparable to the *Lego* or
newspaper tower activities known to many, but on this occasion with
certain crucial constructural elements missing. These would have to be
identified and either made by the participants themselves or acquired
from some outside source. However, these two ideas were abandoned
because of the complexity and possible expense of devising the initial
mechanical problem.

A second possibility considered was a code-breaking exercise.
Participating groups would be invited to write a letter or statement using
a code – of which a specimen was provided. Superficially easy, the code
would be sufficiently complex to prevent participants finding an easy
solution and to provide them with considerable frustration. Only those
with substantial skill and understanding would be able to break it
without seeking assistance, and groups would be penalised according to
the amount of help they were forced to acquire. This possibility had the
additional attraction of being able to be introduced at a variety of levels,

more complex codes for adults and simpler ones for younger and less academically-gifted participants. While not being ruled out, this concept was eventually shelved as it appeared too highly specialised, and it could be difficult at *Review* for individual participants to apply the learning to their own real-life situations.

A third suggestion was of an exercise in which groups would be asked to undertake a task, of a kind actually done by their seniors, for which they might one day apply. Again this task would be one which appeared easy, and participants would learn the hard way that expertise and experience were needed to carry out tasks of this kind. For instance, younger members of a school staff might be asked to prepare a timetable or allocate resources fairly and effectively. This possibility was rejected on three grounds: the complexity and time-consuming nature of the kind of tasks which would be relevant; the fact that it would be unsuitable for younger participants; and the danger of it becoming role-play and thereby losing some of the learning provided by the kind of experiential acitivity being sought.

Seeing the light

At this point, as often happens in writing experiential exercises, an impasse seemed to have been reached. It was proving difficult to find a suitable medium to convey the desired learning process. Discussion with other experts in the field helped to clarify the situation; the suggestion was made that too much emphasis was being placed at this stage on the task to be performed and not enough on the capabilities of the performers. More attention should be given to devising an exercise in which, before the participating groups undertook their task, they would be asked to assess the time and resources they would need to complete it, and, if production was part of the remit, the quantity that they could achieve. Credit would be given more for the accuracy of the forecast than for the achievement of the goal, although both would be important.

In addition, sub-groups could be asked to undertake a complex task or a range of tasks simultaneously so that skills within the group would have to be indentified and jobs allocated to match. The *Review* would be an opportunity to open up discussion on how one assesses capability, and how successful the sub-groups were in doing so. If, as is likely, some sub-groups were unrealistic in their forecasts, why was this so? What skills were they lacking which prevented them from reaching their targets? How might these skills be refined, not in relation to the exercise but in more general terms, so that students were more realistic in matching their attributes and talents to their personal objectives.

Ideas take shape

More thought led eventually to an exercise which could be used in three different ways:

The first was a competitive exercise for individuals in which each was asked to complete as many origami water bombs as he could in 20 minutes. Before the competition started, competitors were given 10 minutes to study the design and the directions and to state how many bombs they believed they could make. If in the 20 minutes they made the precise number of bombs they had estimated, each bomb would score 50 points. If they made more than the stated number, the additional bombs would only score 45 points each. In the same way, if they scored less than they estimated, each bomb would only count for 45 points. Thus the onus was on each individual to think very carefully about his or her potential as accurate forecasting of capability was the key to success. For example, a competitor who forecast that he or she could make eight bombs and did would score 400 points. One who made eight having forecast six would score only 390; and one who forecast eight and only made six would score 290.

The second version of the exercise was identical to the first except that teams of three or four would have the task of making the bombs rather than individuals. This added an extra dimension to the exercise, in that it was now important to identify skills within the team and allocate responsibilities accordingly. More time would need to be allowed for planning, though construction time could remain the same.

The third version was of still greater complexity. Groups now consisted of six to eight; in addition to the water bomb manufacture, two further tasks which required different skills were included. One was the completion of a small jigsaw puzzle, which demanded colour and shape coordination, the other the solution of an analytical problem. In the case of the latter two tasks, the competitors were asked to state how much of the available time they would need to find the solution. They would be penalised for over-estimates or under-estimates in similar fashion to the penalties for miscalculating the water bomb problem. Target times for the tasks would now be 25 minutes, and 15 minutes would be allowed for planning.

Preliminary testing

Before attempting to write the instructions for the exercise, the tutor needed to carry out certain practical tests. One was to make origami water bombs himself to get some idea of how long the task took and the size and type of paper required. A second was to experiment with small jigsaw puzzles to establish what size it was reasonable to expect an individual or small group to complete within 25 minutes. A third was to try out a variety of schemes for scoring to make the competition exciting and demanding for the participants. Only then could the final timing and instructions be decided.

These preliminary tests were carried out, using volunteers where possible, and the exercises were finished for their field testing. *Water Bomb 1* was tested with a mixed-ability fourth year secondary group, *Water Bomb 2* with a 16+ CPVE group, and *Triple Crown* on a group of teachers engaged on an INSET programme run by a University School of Education.

The drafts of the exercises, as used in these field tests, follow. The final versions begin on page 147 in the Exercise Section.

WATER BOMB 1

Objectives	• to help participants realise the importance of a realistic assessment of their skills, capabilities and experience • to stimulate thinking about the matching of these skills, capabilities and experiences to real jobs and career planning
Description	Individuals in competition are asked to calculate how many water bombs they can make in 20 minutes. They then make the bombs and compare the outcome with their forecasts.
Target group	Years 4–5, 6th form, staff
Organisation	One tutor per 15 participants plus observers
Time required	1 hour
Tutor skills	This exercise can be tackled by tutors with little previous experience.
Location	Any room large enough to give the individuals adequate working space.
Materials	One briefing sheet per participant One *Water Bomb* construction sheet per participant Paper for construction (A4 size tests manipulative skills; larger will test use of space)

Tutor's notes

1 Issue each participant with a briefing sheet and a *Water Bomb* construction sheet. Remind them that they have 10 minutes for planning. (*15 minutes*)

2 Collect in declaration tear-off strips. Issue paper. Announce start of construction time. (*20 minutes*)

3 Task ends. Check scores. Declare winner. (*5 minutes*)

4 *Review*
Points which should emerge will include:
a *Planning*
  • Did participants fully understand the scoring system and work out the optimum method of gaining points?
  • How did they calculate the number of bombs they could construct?
  • Did they attempt any practice construction? If so, how?
b *Application*
  • What were the participants' reactions if their calculations were innaccurate?
  • Could they see how their miscalculation arose?
  • How did this exercise relate to planning career structures and applying for jobs? (*20 minutes*)

WATER BOMB 1
Briefing sheet

1 The task

You are about to take part in a competition against the other participants. The competition contains two elements:

a to make as many water bombs as you can in 20 minutes according to the design you have been given;

b to calculate and declare how many bombs you will be able to make in that time.

2 Scoring

a for every water bomb you make you score 50 points

b for every water bomb you make *in excess* of the number you declared, 5 points are deducted

c for every bomb you make *less than* the number you declared, 5 points are deducted

d the participant with the highest score at the end of 20 minutes is the winner

3 Planning

You have 10 minutes in which to plan your course of action. At the end of 10 minutes you are to complete the attached tear-off slip and hand it to your tutor, from whom you will also collect paper for the construction of the bombs. When all the slips have been collected, the tutor will give the signal for the competition to begin.

NAME _____

NUMBER OF BOMBS
TO BE COMPLETED
IN 20 MINUTES _____

WATER BOMB 1
Construction sheet

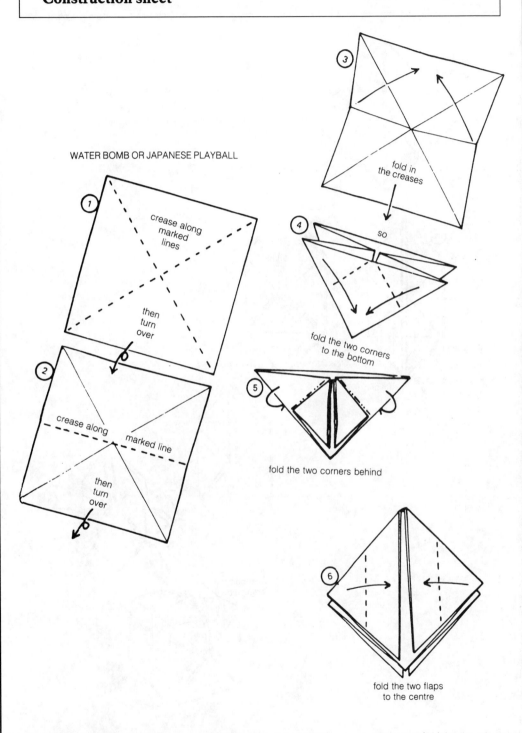

WATER BOMB OR JAPANESE PLAYBALL

1 crease along marked lines

then turn over

2 crease along marked line

then turn over

3 fold in the creases

4 so

fold the two corners to the bottom

5 fold the two corners behind

6 fold the two flaps to the centre

WATER BOMB 1
Construction sheet *continued*

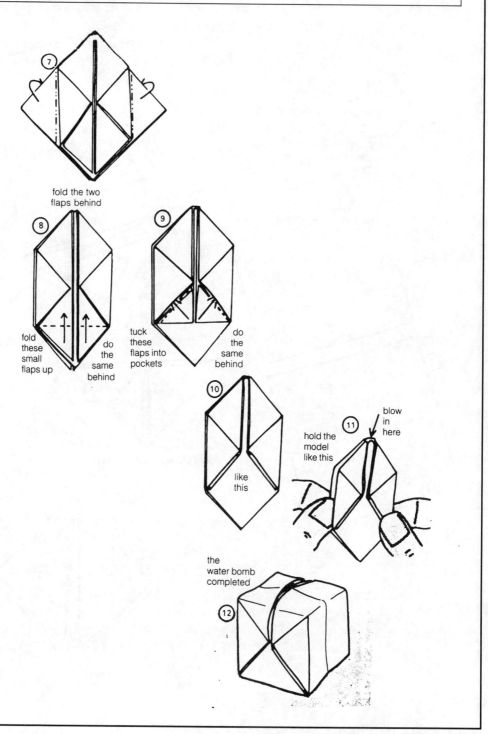

fold the two
flaps behind

fold
these
small
flaps up

do
the
same
behind

tuck
these
flaps into
pockets

do
the
same
behind

like
this

hold the
model
like this

blow
in
here

the
water bomb
completed

WATER BOMB 2

Objectives
- to help participants realise the importance of a realistic assessment of their skills, capabilities and experience
- to stimulate thinking about the matching of these skills, capabilities and experiences to real jobs and career planning.

Description Groups in competition are asked to calculate how many water bombs they can make in 20 minutes. They then make the bombs and compare the outcome with their forecasts.

Target group Years 4–5, 6th form, staff

Organisation Groups of 4. One/two tutors plus two observers

Time required 1 hour

Tutor skills This exercise can be tackled by tutors with little previous experience.

Location Any room large enough to give the individuals adequate working space.

Materials One briefing sheet per group
One *Water Bomb* construction sheet
Paper for construction (A4 size tests manipulative skills; larger will test use of space).

Tutor's notes

1 Issue each participant with a briefing sheet and a *Water Bomb* construction sheet. Remind them that they have 10 minutes for planning. (*15 minutes*)

2 Collect in declaration tear-off strips. Issue paper. Announce start of construction time. (*20 minutes*)

3 Task ends. Check scores. Declare winner. (*5 minutes*)

4 *Review*
Points which should emerge will include:
   a *Planning*
   - Did students fully understand the scoring system and work out the optimum method of gaining points?
   - How did they calculate the number of bombs they could construct?
   - Did they attempt any practice construction? If so, how?
   b *Execution*
   - Did the groups stick to the plan they had made?
   - What happened if they found they were failing to meet their targets?
   - Was any relevant inter-personal behaviour observed?
   c *Application*
   - What were the participants' reactions if their calculations were inaccurate?
   - Could they see how their miscalculation arose?
   - How did this exercise relate to planning career structures and applying for jobs? (*20 minutes*)

WATER BOMB 2
Briefing sheet

1 The task
You are about to take part in a competition against the other groups. The competition contains two elements:

a to make as many water bombs as you can in 20 minutes according to the design you have been given;

b to calculate and declare how many bombs you will be able to make in that time.

2 Scoring

a for every water bomb you make you score 50 points

b for every water bomb you make *in excess* of the number you declared, 5 points are deducted

c for every bomb you make *less than* the number you declared, 5 points are deducted

d the group with the highest score at the end of 20 minutes is the winner

3 Planning
You have 10 minutes in which to plan your course of action. At the end of 10 minutes you are to complete the attached tear-off slip and hand it to your tutor, from whom you will also collect paper for the construction of the bombs. When all the slips have been collected, the tutor will give the signal for the competition to begin.

GROUP MEMBERS _____

NUMBER OF BOMBS
TO BE COMPLETED
IN 20 MINUTES _____

TRIPLE CROWN

Objectives
- to help participants realise the importance of a realistic assessment of their skills, capabilities and experience
- to stimulate thinking about the matching of these skills, capabilities and experiences to jobs and career planning

Description
Groups in competition are asked to undertake simultaneously three tasks requiring different skills. Before commencing the tasks they are required to state what they consider to be the potential of their group either in terms of productivity or of speed of working.

Target group
Staff – possibly 6th form

Organisation
Groups of 6–8. One/two tutors plus one observer per group

Time required
1¼ hours mimimum

Tutor skills
This exercise should only be tackled by tutors with considerable experience.

Location
Any room large enough to give the groups adequate working space.

Materials
For each group:
Two briefing sheets
Two *Water Bomb* construction sheets
Paper (A4 or larger)
One jigsaw (100–150 pieces)
One/two *The Siding* briefing sheets

The Siding is included as a separate activity on page 158 of the Exercise Section.

Tutor's notes

1 Divide the participants into groups of 6–8 and allocate them to working areas within the room. Issue each group with the materials outlined above. (*5 minutes*)

2 Groups work on their plans. Check that they haven't started to construct water bombs or to solve *The Siding* and that they haven't opened the jigsaw box. (*15 minutes*)

3 Collect target sheets. Announce start of working time. Ask observers to time their groups and to note completion of jigsaw and *The Siding* (*25 minutes*)

4 Competition ends. Check scores. Declare winner. (*5 minutes*)

5 *Review*
Groups should be encouraged to consider the following:
   a *Planning*
   - How did the group structure itself and allocate tasks?
   - Was any check made as to the the relevant skills and experience of individual members of the group?
   - Was the scoring system fully understood? Was an attempt made to evaluate the respective scoring potential of each of the three tasks?
   b *The tasks*
   - Did the group keep to its plan? If not, why not?

- When any one of the tasks was completed, what did those involved in it then do? Why?

Any relevant inter-personal behaviour

c *Application*
- How did the group react if its targets proved to be inaccurate?
- Could it see how its miscalculation arose?
- Could it suggest methods of improvement?
- How does this exercise relate to planning career structures and applying for jobs?

1 The task

You are about to take part in a competition against the other groups. The competition includes three elements:

a
- to make as many water bombs as you can in 25 minutes according to the design you have been given;
- to calculate and disclose how many bombs you will be able to make in that time;

b
- to complete a 104-piece jigsaw puzzle;
- to calculate and disclose how long this will take you;

c
- to solve the problem *The Siding*;
- to calculate and disclose how long this will take you.

2 Planning

You have 15 minutes in which to plan your course of action and to calculate your targets. Your tutor has given you two *Water Bomb* construction sheets, a jigsaw and *The Siding*. You may look at these to help your planning, but you may not start on any of the activities or open the jigsaw box until the tutor tells you that the competition has started.

At the end of 15 minutes you are to fill in your target sheet and hand it to the tutor. When he has collected all the target sheets he will give the signal for the competition to begin.

3 Scoring

a Water bomb construction
- for every water bomb you make you score 50 points;
- for every bomb you make *in excess* of the number you declared, 5 points are deducted;
- for every bomb you make *less than* the number you declared, 5 points are deducted.

b Jigsaw
- for completing the jigsaw you score 250 points;
- for completing *within one minute* of your target time there is a bonus of 50 points;
- for every minute *more or less* than this you lose 10 points, whether you have completed the jigsaw or not.

c The Siding
- for solving the problem you score 250 points;

- for a solution *within one minute* of your target time there is a bonus of 50 points;
- for every *minute more or less* than this you lose 10 points whether you have solved the problem or not.

d At the end of 25 minutes the scores from all three activities will be added together and the group with the highest total will be the winner.

TRIPLE CROWN
Target sheet

Group_____

1 Water bombs:

We will construct _____ bombs in 25 minutes.

2 Jigsaw:

We will complete the jigsaw in _____ minutes.

3 The Siding

We will solve the problem in _____ minutes.

After the tests – the final drafts

Water Bomb 1
Water Bomb 1 presented no problems as far as its objectives were concerned. The participants, both during the exercise itself and at *Review*, appreciated the relevance of what they were doing to the process through which they needed to pass when considering their option choices or careers. One or two overestimated their potential because they had made such water bombs before. However, they had failed to recognise that skills wane with the passage of time.

Several of those who underestimated their potential did so because they had not realised that they would become more efficient and quicker as they gained experience. One participant found it impossible to make any bombs at all as the instructions were too complicated. This led naturally to a useful and unhurtful discussion about the fact that many people become aware that they are totally devoid of certain skills. They then have to identify the competency skills which they *have* got and apply them elsewhere.

Successful as the exercise was in fulfilling its objectives, snags and omissions did appear in the briefing sheets and the tutor's notes. These are listed below:

1 During the planning period, most participants had trial runs with any paper they could lay their hands on. This needed clearing away before the exercise proper started.
2 There was no mention of quality control. How well made did a bomb have to be to qualify for points? Mention of this needed to be added to the exercise instructions.
3 Nothing had been said in the instructions about responsibility for timing. It clearly didn't matter who was responsible, in practice, but the tutor did need to be aware that the question would arise.
4 The scoring system needed to be altered for two reasons:
   a) To make the participants think more deeply about it during the planning period. The differential between exactitude and overestimate or underestimate was so slight that many participants ignored it and did not consider the penalties vis-a-vis the advantages of, for instance, an underestimate.
   b) To distinguish between an underestimate and an overestimate, the writer considered (arguably) that it was better for a candidate in career terms to slightly underestimate potential and adjust upwards than to have an exaggerated idea of his own abilities. In real life it was normally an easier adjustment to make. The penalty for overestimating should therefore be greater than that for underestimating.

With these factors taken into account, a final draft of the exercise was produced. This appears on page 148.

Water bomb 2

As in the case of *Water Bomb 1*, *Water Bomb 2* was found to be excellent as an exercise from the point of view of providing interest and involvement. Obviously, the same weaknesses in the instructions as had been noticed in *Water Bomb 1* were again apparent and required attention.

When it came to assessing the relevance of the exercise in fulfilling the stated objectives, it was found that there was only partial success. The participants were able to see the relevance of what they had done to decisions about future career prospects based on perceived skills. However, a far more compelling part of the exercise had been getting them to look at the dynamics of a group at work and to discuss team skills and development. It was decided, therefore, to make this the major aim of the exercise for the future, and to reduce self-awareness to a secondary level. The final draft on page 152 of the Exercise Section, reflects these changes.

Triple crown

An exercise as complicated as *Triple Crown* was bound to produce surprises at the testing stage. The first thing to become immediately apparent was that this exercise was useless in fulfilling its stated objective. The complications of planning and prioritising for the groups were such that they clearly dominated the learning and demanded that more time should be allowed for them. So it was decided to alter the main objective of the exercise to the improvement of planning, prioritising and target setting, and to extend the planning time allowed to 25 minutes. The exercise also helped individuals evaluate their own and group skills, and had much to offer as an activity to be used in assisting discussions on team-building and teamwork.

Scoring was another part of this exercise which demanded alteration. This was inextricably bound up in a complex way with the tactics and planning of the participants. For instance, it was noted that within the total time allowed, the jigsaw could be completed relatively quickly (12 minutes for one group), while *The Siding* needed rather longer. The number of people engaged in these tasks had little relevance to their successful completion; in fact the more people engaged on them, the less effective was often the outcome. Should the scoring system, therefore, be adjusted to allow for the number of people involved or length of time taken? Eventually it was decided to give a bonus for speed in each of these tasks.

It was noted by tutors, though not by participants, that making water bombs was far more productive in point-scoring terms than completing either of the other two tasks. It was surprising, though, that few groups transferred spare personnel into water bomb production after the other two tasks were completed. In fact, as five water bombs equal a completed jigsaw or *The Siding*, a really determined group, having read the rules carefully, would do better to concentrate entirely on water bombs and ignore the other tasks altogether. Attention was given to the possibility of evening up the scores for the different activities, but in the end it was decided that this opportunity for tactical imagination was valuable and should not be disturbed. In any case, the introduction of a bonus for those completing the jigsaw or *The Siding* swiftly should act as some compensation, and tutors can always adjust the scoring system as they think appropriate, in order to introduce some of the issues posed by competition between groups discussed in the previous chapter.

Triple crown, therefore, emerged with a different set of objectives and some alteration to its scoring system, but otherwise basically unchanged.

8 Anatomy of an exercise

Characteristics of a good exercise

The most important characteristic of a good exercise is that it should be flexible. The more prescriptive the objectives, the more precise the instructions, the less varied and extensive are the outcomes. A good exercise will be presented to a tutor in such a form that it can be used with individuals from as wide an age and interest range as possible; that access to it can be gained at different academic and intellectual levels; that a tutor with particular skills and perception of needs can add to it or subtract from it as circumstances demand; and that it can be used with groups of differing sizes.

Certain constraints will be inevitable – basic objectives, minimum numbers, essential equipment, available time, for example – but a good exercise will be open-ended in the scope that is left for participants to be responsible for their own organisation, structure and behaviour. While designers of the exercises will have had clear ideas in mind as to what their exercises are aiming to achieve, the learning which emerges will be that appropriate to the occasion, and no two occasions are the same. If the tutors embark upon exercises having decided on the outcome before they start, they will stifle the natural learning process which will be at work on that particular day with that particular group of students.

In short, what experienced tutors require of a good exercise is a set of basic aims, an outline structure and the details of the necessary minimum equipment. From their own 'kit-bags' of experience they will then ensure that as far as possible there is good learning for at least the majority of the participants. Less experienced tutors may need more guidance, but too much direction inhibits learning.

The Trading Game

The aim of this chapter is to examine one exercise which has been used with conspicuous success according to the criteria used in this book, to describe the flexibility which exists within it and the consequent variety of the learning which can be derived from it, and to show how the comparative rigidity of its structure and instructions can be an inhibiting factor if tutors allow themselves to be bound by them.

The Trading Game was originally published by Christian Aid in 1982, and revised in 1986. For the purposes of this chapter it is discussed in its original form. The changes that were made do not affect the comments made about it as an activity. In the introduction the writers state that 'the game is intended to help the players understand more clearly how trade can affect the prosperity of a country'. The stated aims add that 'the game is designed to illustrate how the process of trade can benefit and hinder the economic development of different communities or countries . . . Players will almost certainly want to talk about their experiences during the playing of the game and this is turn should lead to a broader discussion about trading relationships'.

This aim could prove highly specific and very limiting. The possibility of behaviour being influenced as a result of the exercise is not mentioned, and even in the back-up material, the changes that are presupposed are to do with the students' perceptions of fairness and injustice in the existence, use and exploitation of the resources of the world and in their moral attitudes towards their own wealth. It will be shown later that the potential for learning in the exercise is vast and covers a far wider range of experience and behaviour than that described above.

Playing the game – The 'Do'

The *Doing* aspect of *The Trading Game* involves the participants working in groups to manufacture paper shapes. These have to be produced accurately using proper tools, ie scissors, compasses, set square and protractors.

The limiting factor is that different groups have different quantities of 'tools' and 'raw materials', ie paper. The groups, therefore, equate to different groups of countries in the modern world.

Grade A groups represent industrial countries with plenty of tools but limited raw materials. Grade B and Grade C represent two levels of lesser-developed countries with varying quantities of tools and raw materials. Students will not even realise the value of some of the latter (eg coloured sticky paper).

Once manufacturing commences, groups barter and trade with each

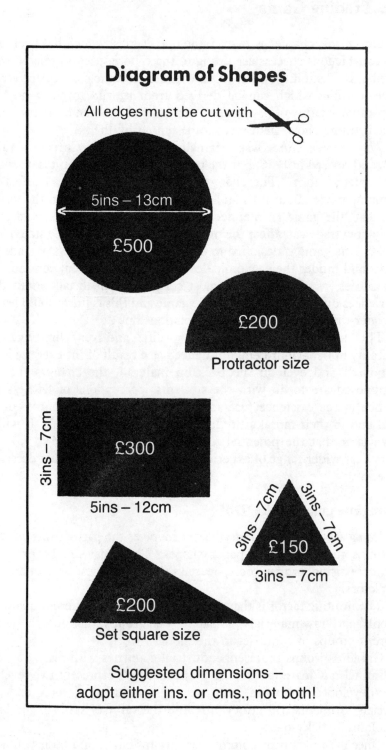

Diagram of Shapes

All edges must be cut with ✂

5ins – 13cm

£500

£200

Protractor size

3ins – 7cm

£300

5ins – 12cm

3ins – 7cm   3ins – 7cm

£150

3ins – 7cm

£200

Set square size

Suggested dimensions –
adopt either ins. or cms., not both!

Grade A – Two Sets of the following:	2 pairs of scissors ✄ 2 rulers ╱ 1 compass ⋀ 1 set square ▶ 1 protractor ◪ 1 sheet of paper ◗ 6 'pound notes' £100 4 lead pencils ╲
Grade B – Two Sets of the following:	10 sheets of paper ◆ 1 sheet sticky paper ▬ 2 'pound notes' £100

	Number of Players	Resource-set	Some suggested country names for groups
1	👥👥👥👥👥👥	Grade A	USA UK
2	👥👥👥👥👥👥	Grade A	ITALY FRANCE
3	👥👥👥👥👥	Grade B	INDIA BRAZIL
4	👥👥👥👥👥	Grade B	NIGERIA PERU
5	👥👥👥👥	Grade C	TANZANIA KENYA
6	👥👥👥👥	Grade C	BURMA GHANA

other to acquire the tools and raw materials they need. As shapes are manufactured, they are lodged with the Banker, who keeps a record of each group's wealth as it grows. During the course of the exercise the tutor can influence the proceedings by altering the value of the paper shapes, thus changing the value of the various 'tools'; by supplying extra raw materials to individual groups; and by revealing secretly to all or some of the groups which do not possess coloured sticky paper that 'if they stick small squares of it to their products they will be worth four times the original value'.

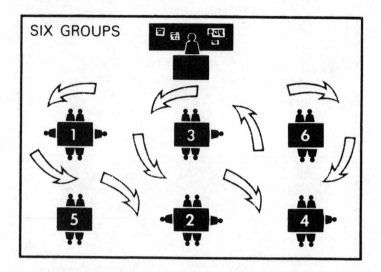

Instructions are given to the tutor as to the layout of the room and the size of individual groups. Again, it will be seen later that the precision of these can detract from the learning inherent in the exercise. The objectives and values of the game are simple and clearly defined. They have to be read out to the groups by the tutor.

2. Now read out the objectives and rules of the game to the players. These are as follows:

"The objective of each group is to make as much wealth for itself as possible by using the materials given to it. No other materials can be used. The wealth is made by manufacturing paper shapes. The goods you are going to manufacture are the shapes shown on the Diagram of Shapes. Each shape has its own value as shown on the Diagram and these paper shapes are given to the *banker* in batches for checking and crediting to your bank account. You can manufacture as many shapes as you like — the more you make the wealthier you will be."

"There are just four simple rules:

● All the shapes need to be cut with clean sharp edges using scissors and must be of the exact size shown — the shapes are taken to the banker for your account.

● You can only use the materials that have been given out.

● There is to be no physical force used during the game.

● The leader represents the United Nations and will intervene in any disagreements."

Experiences with the exercise

As has been said earlier, the potential for experiential learning in *The Trading Game* is enormous, but the structure as outlined above can be a limiting factor. In particular, the aim 'to illustrate how the process of trade can benefit and hinder the economic development of different communities or countries', can, if allowed to dominate, stifle much of this potential. Once one broadens the horizon of the exercise with a view to exploring economic awareness, values, inter-group and personal behaviour and the workings of the group themselves, the possibilities become apparent. There are a number of ways in which this can be done, but the most important factor is to develop that state of mind which is determined to preserve the open-endedness of the exercise at all costs. Some of the methods involved are described below.

1 Allowing groups to select themselves

The original instructions for the exercise indicate two groups in each of the grades. Grade A groups have six members each, Grade B five and Grade C four. The reason for this disposition of participants is not clear.

However, if the groups are permitted to select themselves, subject to a minimum size of three (or even two) and a possible maximum as well, all kinds of new variables are revealed. In the first place, there is the simple problem of the self-selection itself. The way in which the groups came together will provide a major topic for discussion at the *Review* stage of the exercise. How did the sexes divide between the groups? Were they based on normal friendship groups or associations? What happened to loners or isolates?

Such discussion will be extended if, for whatever reason, groups have decided to join forces and pool resources during the course of the exercise itself. It sometimes happens, for instance, that two Grade A groups decide to combine or that a Grade A group joins with a Grade C one. The reasons for such an alliance and the effect of the alliance both on the productive capacity of the groups and on the participants as individuals will provide valuable material for the *Review*.

Then there is the question of whether the number in a group affected the group's performance, and whether this was for the better or the worse. In addition to discussing whether Grade A groups are likely to be more or less successful than Grade B and Grade C groups, participants may want to examine why a Grade A group with six members did better or worse than one with four. If there was a difference, was it the result of the different numbers in the group or of the skills of the group members – or both? Was the nature of the task a significant factor? Do we now set the same groups a different task to find out? All these possibilities emerge once a self-selection policy is adopted which allows variety of size among the groups.

2 Adding additional groups

On one occasion, in an area of high unemployment, a group was added to the exercise and given neither 'tools' nor 'raw materials' but an empty envelope. The behaviour of this group was interesting. After a moment of puzzlement and the expected suggestion to the tutor that some mistake must have been made in the organisation of the exercise, the group hit on the strategy of siezing the posters on the wall which showed the dimensions of the shapes to be manufactured. Unfortunately for their plan, several groups had already made copies of these and so their action was ineffective. At this juncture, the 'unemployed' group seemed nonplussed and unable to devise any alternative strategy apart from requesting a loan from the bank – which was refused!

In the subsequent *Review* a number of other possibilities were suggested. These included attempting to beg or borrow from other groups, and offering their manpower elsewhere – either collectively or individually. Feelings also came to the fore. The 'unemployed' described how they had felt angry, frustrated, inadequate, and tempted to dishonesty. Other 'employed' groups felt that they would have helped had they appreciated their less fortunate colleagues' situation. This claim was treated by the 'unemployed' with scepticism.

The addition of this unresourced group clearly gave a new dimension to the exercise and caused the tutor subsequently to consider whether other groups with special needs, resources or skills could be introduced where the situation was appropriate. For instance, a group with the ability to mass-produce one or more of the shapes, but with no 'raw materials' at all, could add new perspectives to the negotiating which normally takes place.

3 Not structuring the working environment

The diagram giving instructions about the layout of the room states that 'each of the six groups needs a table or desk as a work surface and a chair or two for each group would be useful'. While this is undeniably true, there is much to be said for allowing a group to discover the fact for itself. It is surprising how often a group will put up unnecessarily with inadequate working conditions which could easily be remedied. Groups will fail to note the flexible nature of much furniture; will put up with surplus chairs and other equipment getting in their way instead of removing them; and will work on the floor rather than bring a table from another part of the room. This is especially true of many schoolchildren who have apparently been conditioned to classrooms where the furniture must not be moved for fear of disturbing the caretaker! The realisation that boundaries are there to be tested (in this case that tables can often be found in other rooms) is a valuable piece of learning, and opens up the whole question of the importance of the working environment for the successful completion of the task.

4 Maintaining flexibility of aims

One tutor using *The Trading Game* ended the *Review* by asking all participants to list what they felt they had learnt under the following headings:

> Geography
> Economic awareness
> Values
> How groups work
> Myself
> Anything else

He had appreciated that this exercise contained so much potential learning that he did not wish to restrict this in any way by focusing the participants' thoughts too much on any one aspect. On this occasion he was working with a group of highly-motivated, intelligent and skilled adults. He might not have encouraged quite such an open-ended approach with younger or less-able students who could have been helped by having their thoughts guided towards one or two areas only. Time limitations could also have a bearing on the range of the learning to be attempted in the *Review*.

This said, it is worth noting some of the learning that has emerged at various times under each of these headings:

Geography
Students have admitted to having their awareness of the divide between North and South heightened and even to having become more familiar with the actual geographical location of individual countries. The importance of raw materials and the relationship between their exploitation and the need for conservation are other topics of discussion.

Economic awareness
The whole pattern of trade, the effect of changing market values and the problem of international debt have been factors to emerge. Adult participants have suggested that the possibility of credit from the Bank and of giving value to 'raw materials' would be useful occasional variants, which could be added to the exercise. Younger students have noted the importance of quality control and the fact that there is virtually nothing that does not have some value if the right purchaser can be found.

On occasion groups have attempted to cheat the Banker by presenting shapes which have not been produced by proper 'tools' but which have been cleverly executed with other devices. Relative to world trade, these activities are analogous to some products from countries like Taiwan; the issue of cheaply-provided substitutes can be discussed during *Review*.

Values

On one occasion the tutor noted a girl student removing paper from another group, who had all left their base unattended in the excitement of the negotiation that was in progress. Later, still unnoticed, she returned the paper again.

In *Review* this fact was not revealed, so the tutor described what he had seen and asked for an explanation. The student replied that her group was in grave difficulty because of lack of 'raw materials' so she took the paper, but later she returned it because 'she knew it was wrong to steal'. Subsequent questions revealed that several male students had also 'stolen' paper, but had not returned it because of the importance of winning. A useful discussion on values and gender issues followed naturally.

How groups work

The whole process of the exercise will provide relevant material here. Topics such as leadership, roles, sharing information, communication skills, organisation and structure will emerge.

Among younger students it is not uncommon for physically powerful participants to bully the rest of a group into submitting to their plans. At a more subtle level, one older group was coerced by a dominant but entirely self-appointed leader into doing nothing, on the erroneous assumption that they would be given credit in the final account for keeping 'raw materials' intact (St Luke, Ch 19, V 21!). Discussion of this revealed that, as the exercise was drawing towards its close, the other members of the group began to waver in their resolve, but that they still could not bring themselves to break their leader's hold over them. Not surprisingly, they were the least successful trading group.

Myself

As experiential learning is all about changing behaviour, participants are bound to learn more about themselves, their strengths and weaknesses. It may be the student who cannot act dishonestly, or who has an in-built determination to win at all costs, or the adult who cannot throw off the hold of a dominant though misguided leader. The unemployed group were able to talk openly about their reactions to their predicament and relate these to people who were suffering similarly in reality. Experience shows that these reactions are likely to be recalled at a later date when similar situations arise. In this way students gain a greater insight into their strengths, potential or weaknesses in such skills as leadership, communication, coping with failure, giving feedback, negotiation and so on. They are in a position to modify their behaviour on subsequent occasions, though it does not of course follow that they will actually be able to do so.

Much of this learning about self will not be disclosed in the *Review* because of its highly personal nature, and it would be wrong of the tutor to press for such disclosures. However, the learning cannot help being there, and it is hoped that it will be used by the student to modify behaviour. Students indeed often report such changes immediately after the event, but it is hard to make long-term evaluations of behavioural change because it is both difficult and costly to observe in an objective fashion.

9 'The great outdoors'

The place of outdoor activities

All the experiential learning discussed so far and all the activities described have assumed that tutors will be working indoors and will be subject to the discipline of a timetable which will restrict the length of the exercises or activities which can be undertaken.

However, readers will be aware that we have in this country a tradition of outdoor experiential learning stretching back at least as far as the formation of the Boy Scout movement in the first decade of the present century. As we shall see, the aims of much of the early work were largely different from those which underline the experiential learning we have been describing, but there is overlap. From these origins has evolved a whole range of developmental activities based on the outdoors and owned by such bodies as Outward Bound, Brathay Hall Trust and Endeavour Training.

Kurt Hahn

The most significant figure in the earlier developments of outdoor education was probably Kurt Hahn, the moving spirit behind Gordonstoun, Atlantic College and Outward Bound. His major aim, however, was not the systematic and purposeful development of the whole person through active learning but the more limited one of character building designed to produce leaders noted for their spiritual and physical health and their dedication to service. Much of this was achieved through an emphasis on athletic achievement and on the requirement for students to undertake community service. At Gordonstoun this consisted of a choice between coastguard work, a fire service and mountain rescue. In those early days the ethos was largely directive and a rigid timetable was in existence which allowed little free time, certainly not enough for review of the type essential for successful experiential learning.

Current philosophy

Contemporary exponents of outdoor experiential learning have moved in the direction described in this book. Putnam (1988) in *A Rationale for Outward Bound* cites among other aims:

> to encourage change and to help each participant more fully to achieve self-knowledge and understanding of others.

> Central to this process is the responsibility of the participant, helped by his companions and the staff, to review and evaluate continuously what occurs during and following the course.

> The outcome lies in a changed self-concept, enhanced self-knowledge, a changed understanding of others, greater adaptability to change and an increased capacity to learn from future experience.

The additional features of some outdoor experiential learning are the physical challenge, the attempt to stretch the whole person and to help participants to reach the limits of which they are capable. This factor, however, is not invested with extreme significance by all practitioners. Indeed, if it were, it could present an unhelpful image of experiential learning to participants who were physically incompetent or handicapped.

Extra dimensions provided by outdoor education

Given that the basic concepts of experiential learning in the outdoors are the same as those of learning conducted in the more restricted indoor environment, namely: planning according to the client's perceived needs, an activity and a review, including appropriate follow-up arrangements organised by the tutor, what extra dimensions and advantages can be provided by 'the great outdoors'? A number of these are postulated and for the purposes of convenience they can be grouped under three main headings.

1 The holistic nature of the experience

Most indoor activities are by their very nature restricted in space, and therefore variety. Outdoor activity is essentially different. The geographical area which can be employed can cover many square miles of highly varied terrain, including mountain and water. The time generally though not invariably required is substantially greater, varying from half a day to the inside of a week, even though the amount achieved in a single mountain day is likely to be greater than would be achieved during an equivalent time indoors.

The potential activities that can be included increase in proportion, and a wide variety of objectives and sub-objectives are available in the same exercise. For instance, an activity which starts off as a raft-building exercise can then develop into a 'treasure hunt' involving such varied skills as propelling the raft, map reading and code breaking. Sub-objectives may include selection of a leader, control of time, planning the food requirements for the duration of the exercise together with the necessary cooking, and ensuring the availability of other materials and back up.

Given this variety of objectives, the variety of experience available to participants is obvious. Not only is a whole range of different terrain, weather and physical activity provided by nature, but a variety of practical experience and skill development is also required in such exercises as described above. In addition there is the opportunity for emotional and aesthetic experience (as described in section 3 below). There are few indoor activities which could combine the affective domain with psychometric skills of so many kinds alongside management attributes like planning, problem solving, communication and decision making.

This in its turn provides participants with a wide variety of choice and avoidance. In the *Review* it will be possible to learn extensively from what students choose, how and why. Did the group use fully and sensibly the skills existing in its members? What feelings and emotions emerged and what effect did they have? Did individuals avoid certain activities or aspects of the exercise and, if so, why? There is enormous opportunity to explore the holistic nature of the experiences and for individuals to discover the extent to which they entered into them.

2   The heightening of reality

Because many indoor experiential activities contain a substantial degree of artificiality in their design, it is easier for participants to withdraw from real commitment to the exercise, giving lack of realism as a pretext. 'What is the point of making a tower from newspapers, or a Lego man?' 'Why work out the most appropriate design of make-believe fire extinguishers for a mythical factory?' While such objections almost invariably mark some far deeper apprehensions, even the most skilled trainer may find it impossible to persuade a student to acknowledge this during the *Review*, let alone reveal it.

In outdoor experiential activity, on the other hand, the practical nature of the exercise and the physical challenge involved make such evasions difficult, if not impossible. If the task of a group is building a raft, following a route on the ground by map and compass, or crossing some physical obstacle, the reality of success or failure is clear. Either the task has been achieved or it has not. Either you took an identifiable part in the group operations or you did not. These are not things that can be easily fudged.

In addition to this we are all probably aware of the way in which a physical achievement, perhaps beyond anything we would have expected from ourselves, lives with us for years to come. The successful completion of a long-distance walk or the climbing of a substantial mountain are achievements which we are likely to be talking about months later. Equally, and perhaps surprisingly, the walk which had to be called off before it was finished because of extremes of weather, or the mountain which refused to be conquered, live on equally vividly in our memory.

Add to this the fact that many outdoor activities include an element of perceived risk and the reality and memorability of the experience are heightened still further. Even though the safety precautions will be as near fool-proof as possible, and all participants will be protected by safety ropes or nets or whatever is appropriate, as you set off on your abseil or your death slide the perception of risk will be very strong. The success, failure and risks of indoor experiential exercise are less easy to define and quantify and less likely to be an on-going source of learning for any protracted period of time.

3   The outdoors as a medium of reflection

Most of us will be aware of the effect that the world of nature can have on our emotions and senses. We have all, at one time or another, been affected by the beauty and awesome power of a great waterfall, by a sensational sunset or mountainscape, by the delicate charm of a flower or a butterfly or by the sound of a running stream, or water breaking on the shore. Experts in outdoor experiential learning suggest that as our senses and emotions are heightened in this way, the natural environment in which we are working adds to our ability to reflect on what we have been doing and to renew the learning that has taken place. At Brathay, as described later in the chapter, older participants may be asked to withdraw individually to any place of their choice in the vicinity in order to spend time on such reflection on their own, and participants have testified to the value of this process. Even younger or less-mature members, though unable to articulate their responses so explicitly, can find that their learning is reinforced in this way.

Caveats

Beside the extra dimension which can be given to experiential learning by the use of the outdoors must be placed two warnings. The first is the danger of using the outdoors for the outdoors' sake. Being outside is naturally associated with many pleasant things, from walking or caravanning at week-ends to holidays and family outings. It is generally attactive to be out of doors and for many people it provides a contrast with the normal workplace. There is a temptation, therefore, to be outdoors simply because it is a pleasant place to be rather than because our learning will be enhanced by the extra dimension provided. Given the factors involved in working outdoors, such as time and expense, which will be described later in the chapter, there is nothing to be gained and the likelihood of unnecessary complication if the outdoors is used without specific reason and where no enhancement of the learning will result.

The second danger is an over-emphasis on the physical and a macho image which can be highly off-putting to those whose age, build or co-ordination may hamper them in activities which make considerable physical demands. The skilled tutor always pays particular attention to the middle-aged, clumsy and apprehensive. An initial enquiry will always be made of participants about any physical disability they may have, and they will be reassured that at no stage will any attempt be made to make them uncomfortable physically (other than from tiredness) and that it is their responsibility to say if at any time they don't wish to take part. At the same time they will be reminded that the exercises are group activities in which the team is encouraged to use its strengths and weaknesses as appropriate. In the *Review*, emphasis needs to be laid on any apprehensions which have been overcome, in order that the learning will be applied to other activities and to the participants' places of work.

Constraints on outdoor experiential learning

1   Time

As has already been stated, the majority of outdoor exercises require considerably longer than the normal session of a school or college. Activities may vary in length from an afternoon to a week which will make them difficult to accommodate as a routine part of the normal timetable. However, there are a number of ways in which this difficulty can be overcome. Some of these are listed below:

a) Arranging special half-day, one-day or one-week modules, conducted on a one-off basis outside the normal timetable. The one-week modules benefit from being residential.

b) Converting all or part of the existing fieldwork or outdoor pursuits programme to developmental experiential activity either as an alternative or as an extra dimension to the existing programme.

c) Using some of the mini-exercises (two examples of which are given below).

2 Expense

It is undeniable that outdoor experiential learning will be more expensive than that done indoors. Unless a school or college is luckily placed geographically, there are often transport costs to be considered. Most activities require specialist equipment and even the minimum of proper weatherproof clothing and boots costs a considerable sum of money. Equipment for climbing, water activities and exercises involving constructional tasks will add substantially to this. If a residential programme is being undertaken, there is the cost of accommodation and food to be considered also. Once again, using mini-exercises will help here as they are comparatively cheap to set up and can be used over and over again. On their own, however, they will not be a substitute for more major learning activities.

3 Maintenance and safety of equipment

Much of the equipment used in outdoor experiential learning requires regular maintenance and checks for safety. Residential centres have on their staff experts who maintain and check fixed equipment and who ensure that boats, ropes, life-jackets and the like are up to the required standard. It is unlikely that a school or college will own much equipment of this kind, but there is still the responsibility to ensure that weatherproof personal clothing is adequate, that torches have batteries and that compasses are in working order. In this area of experiential learning, where there are often likely to be risks, no chance can be taken.

4 Safety and control

Any outdoor activity always requires a greater degree of control than an exercise which takes place in a classroom or hall. At the most basic level, the fact that a room is a circumscribed area means that control within it becomes far simpler. However, much outdoor work actually requires participants to move over a wide area in such exercises as map reading or treasure hunts, or to take part in activities with a substantial degree of risk such as climbing or watermanship. Staffing these exercises is clearly more demanding in numbers of personnel required than normal school or college staffing ratios permit; for activities involving risk, tutors with qualifications in the relevant pursuits will be needed. Even for fell walking or map reading, where groups are to work unsupervised, the amount of preparation demanded of tutors is formidable. Route maps and check points must be agreed, the weather conditions and wind and chill factor must be taken into account, and proper equipment and procedures for first aid and emergency must be available. Even the mini-exercise may have some risk factor and safety precautions will need to have been thought out and made clear to the participants.

The mini-exercise

Given the constraints described above, it may well seem impossible for schools and colleges to engage in outdoor experiential learning except on the one-off or fieldwork basis. The mini-exercise, however, may give the opportunity to operate on a comparatively small scale without impossible constraints of time, expense or supervision.

Two such mini-exercises are described on pages 195 and 196 of the Exercise Section. It will be noted that they can easily be fitted into the duration of a normal school or college session, though time for the *Review* may be short, and that the equipment needed is in one case negligible (eggs, sellotape, balloons) and in the other not complicated or particularly expensive. However, supervision may still present a problem as groups cannot realistically be bigger than four or five; in one example there is also a safety factor which must be observed. It is unlikely that any tutor could supervise more than two groups and only then if they were in close proximity.

Brathay Hall Trust – a case study

Origins

The Brathay Hall Trust was founded by Francis Scott in 1946. His original aim, much in the tradition of Kurt Hahn and the early outdoor pioneers, was 'the opening of young people's minds to the possibilities of living adventurously in the world of physical activity as well as in the world of spirit'. He started from a fairly limited baseline, providing young people in industry with the opportunity of widening their horizons through new experiences and challenge. Soon the Brathay Exploration Group was formed and a Field Study Centre established. The latter ran courses in Biology, Geography and related subjects for schools and universities until 1986. From such beginnings Brathay has grown until it now caters for the widest possible range of clients from industry, commerce, education and the public sector who are looking for development training.

The site

Brathay is situated near Ambleside in its own extensive grounds on the north-west shore of Lake Windermere. The house itself is Georgian and has been adapted specifically for its present purpose. An adjacent modern building houses group rooms, theatre, dining room and a visitors' guest wing, containing rooms for from 4 to 10 people. On the technical side there is a boathouse with seven large whaler rowing boats, a canoe fleet and power/safety boats; a fully-equipped central equipment store and workshops; and kit lockers for the outdoor and specialist clothing and equipment which is provided for each working group. Altogether, Brathay can accommodate 80 clients at any one time and requires a tutorial staff of 20 to run the establishment.

Clientele

Brathay's aim is to show maximum flexibility in what it offers. It is constantly re-assessing where the needs are to which it must respond, and is fully geared to providing 'tailor-made' courses of development training as requested by individual clients. Its extensive range of residential activities is presented through two divisions, the Centre for Leadership and Development Training which caters for the needs of industry and business, and the Youth Development Programme. In addition, there is an increasing demand for tutors and training advisers available to work on projects and training programmes away from Brathay.

The Centre for Leadership and Development Training offers both open and contract courses. The former include a *Personal leadership and development* course for those in their late teens and early twenties, which aims to develop an understanding of personal leadership, self-confidence, an increased awareness of self and understanding of others, and skills in working with other people; a *Leadership in action* course for those in their early to late twenties, providing practice in different styles of leadership, a study of group dynamics and opportunities for self-assessment and for developing self confidence in handling people; and a *Manager in action* course, for the older age groups, coupling leadership in various contexts and developing skills in getting results through people.

Contract work involves designing packages to form part of an organisation's training strategy. Visits may take place from the client organisation to Brathay and vice versa, and a Training Proposal and draft programme are drawn up, together with an agreement on content, timing and costs. The type of training involved includes team development and the development of senior staff.

The Youth Development Programme has worked with an exceptionally wide range of young people, mainly in the 14–20 age range. These have included schoolpupils – both those sponsored by Project Trident and those involved in GCSE environmental education programmes; trainees on the Youth Training Scheme; young unemployed adults from local education authorities in both urban and rural areas; young employees on company-sponsored programmes; young people with special needs as a result of learning difficulties or disablement; and a whole range of adults who work with young people.

Aims

Brathay's central purpose is described as 'to provide learning opportunities through which people may realise and harness their potential and so make realistic plans for improving both the quality of their lives and their contribution to our society and the world in which we live'. This aim is based on three fundamental principles:

1 A belief in the dignity and potential of every individual.
2 A commitment to learning that leads to personal and social development.
3 A confidence in training approaches that give individuals responsibility for their own development and encourage understanding of the learning process.

It is hoped that all who attend courses at Brathay will increase their self-confidence and self-awareness, will develop greater resourcefulness and capability, and, in addition to widening their horizons, broadening their experience and extending their capacity for enjoyment, will acquire a sense of achievement. They will improve their understanding of others, and will both gain a realisation of the need for good communication and enhance their own personal communication skills. Above all, the whole experience, with the opportunity for reflection which it provides, will assist them in forming and developing true values and perspectives, and will help them to formulate real plans for the future.

Some typical activities

As development training is only possible through experiential learning, all courses are based on the concept of learning by doing. Projects are designed to encourage leadership, teamwork, planning and good communications, and full use is made of all the facilities described, indoors as well as outdoors. Course members will normally encounter new experiences and acquire new skills from a wide range of activities which can include screen-painting, drama, conservation, boatwork, raft building and mountaineering. As is to be expected, there is a strong emphasis on the *Review* process, and a substantial amount of time is devoted to this. In a five-day course for supervisors, designed to enhance confidence and self-reliance, to develop skills in making things happen, to increase awareness of self and understanding of others, and to make specific plans to put into practice at work, between two and four hours per full working day are allocated to *Review* and individual working time.

The course in question is an interesting example of the variety of activity provided and the methods of tuition used. The course assembles at lunchtime on Monday and the remainder of the first day is spent in preparation, in exploring aims and methods, in briefing and in gathering essential outdoor equipment. Individual working time gives the opportunity for groups to begin a Development Record for each person on the course.

Tuesday is a Mountain Day in which groups are largely responsible for their own programming and maintenance during a mountain walk. Although this day is unlikely to be exceptionally demanding physically, it does place demands on the participants for setting their own objectives, team building, communicating, navigating and so on. The tutor will only intervene on the grounds of safety. The *Review* in the evening allows members to identify whether their plans for the day were over- or under-ambitious, to discuss how they set their objectives, and to examine how people coped, how they helped out when problems arose, how competently they learned skills such as navigation and whether existing skills were transferred.

Wednesday sees two shorter exercises, a Strategy Project and a Design Project, and the start of a major exercise which involves the night out and also half of Thursday. The Strategy Project is a planning-type exercise lasting little over an hour and finishing before breakfast! It is a simple map reading competition between the groups, requiring quick decision making, accurate navigation, strict time discipline and the setting of realistic targets for individuals. The Design project after breakfast involves small groups developing ideas using silk screen painting techniques (eg designing and producing tee-shirts) and making a presentation to the rest of the course.

The major exercise lasts from 7.30 on the Wednesday evening till 1.00 pm on the Thursday. It may well involve the construction of a craft capable of carrying a stated number of passengers on the lake, followed by a 'treasure hunt' in the vessel searching for clues in and around the lake itself. Throughout this exercise the groups are self-resourcing, and again tutors will only intervene if there is a threat to safety.

Friday morning is largely devoted to making action plans for the return to work before the course disperses at lunchtime.

This course is typical of the work undertaken at Brathay. It shows clearly the variety of activity used during a single learning package, the emphasis placed on personal responsibility and self-awareness, the importance of inter-dependence and team skills, the key position of the *Review,* and the aim to ensure that individuals return to their places of work with practical plans and not just good intentions. It also highlights the added scope and dimension that outdoor activity gives to experiential learning when compared with activities that can only be offered indoors.

Training the tutors

The basic skills required by a tutor engaged in outdoor experiential activity will be no different from those needed by tutors in more traditional active learning indoors. The tutor is still the enabler, responsible for setting up the learning situation within which personal development can take place. Interventions will be as few as possible as he or she will be aiming on every occasion for the participants to take responsibility for their own development and to draw their own conclusions in *Review*. The tutor will, therefore, act as a third party, a 'mirror', keeping the process moving without influencing it in any subjective way. He or she is also responsible for ensuring the 'safety' of the participants if they proceed too far down a path where emotional distress is likely.

There are, however, additional skills needed by those working in the outdoors. Some of these are technical – specific professional skills such as climbing and watermanship together with knowledge of the safety requirements involved in such activities and expertise in first aid. There are also those skills which enable a participant, who may be unnerved by the prospect of a physical activity which appears unfamiliar, demanding and ostensibly dangerous, to gain the confidence to take part or alternatively to withdraw without excessive damage to his ego. These skills consist of a calm, confidence-building, assured professionalism combined with a shrewd sensitivity.

Brathay endeavours to nurture this combination of skills in its tutors by a training programme which consists of three elements:

1 A knowledge of training methods and models, the theory base from which the Trust works in all its activities, whether indoors or outdoors;
2 The facilitative skills of working with individuals and groups;
3 The practical skills related to ensuring safety outdoors.

The first two of these are, of course, the skills which should be part and parcel of the equipment of all tutors involved in experiential learning and development training, though all-too-often the first is neglected at the expense of the second. The third element consists of the skills which are particularly important for those working outdoors.

10 Triumphs and disasters

Estimating success in transmissive teaching

Experiential and transmissive styles each have an important part to play in the learning process. A transmissive style is invaluable when a corpus of information has to be passed from teacher to learner, because only the first level of learning – memory – is demanded of students. If formulae need to be learned and applied, for example, then the second and third levels – understanding and application – can be achieved.

The success of this style can be estimated quite quickly in a number of ways: an algebraic or geometric formula successfully applied to the solution of a particular problem in the classroom or examination; historical data memorised so as to give an accurate and logical account of the causes and course of, say, the First World War; vocabulary, grammar and syntax adequately learned and then applied (in a limited way) in a competent translation into English.

The conventional method of estimating success with transmissive styles is the traditional examination paper which, when passed with sufficiently high marks, shows that a candidate has grasped the knowledge which has been transmitted. Because this style of learning is based on a simple didactive model in which a teacher imparts a knowledge to learner, which in turn is memorised and reapplied, success can be measured without too much difficulty and too much controversy, provided that the constraints of the model are accepted.

The main problem is that of the closed cycle. In many situations memorising occurs to satisfy examiners, while understanding and application are tested within the context of an examination. It is very difficult to assess whether the fourth level of learning – transfer – has occurred, in which a student is enabled to use the knowledge or skill acquired in new and different situations away from the classroom, lecture-room or examination.

Success in experiential learning

Estimating success in experiential learning is a totally different and far more complex procedure. To begin with, it is seldom – if ever – quantifiable. Learning which has resulted through a transmission from tutor to student can be tested through examination procedures – 75% indicates a high level of success, 50% a satisfactory level and so on. The procedure can be portrayed as objective, provided the limitations of the whole learning and examination processes are accepted.

This is not possible with experiential learning. An exercise or activity may be designed to enhance students' understanding of the qualities and skills required for leadership, at the same time as demonstrating the individual needs of students in this respect. No instant, quantifiable measure of success is possible. At best it will be hoped that when a similar activity is undertaken in the future, or when a chance for leadership occurs in a participant's daily life at home or at work, an enhanced understanding of skill in leadership will be displayed. But there is no way of measuring this, and if it is a real-life situation, no tutor will be present even to observe it.

Second, the learning will not be the same for all participants and therefore an estimate of success cannot be identical either. In a translation from a foreign language in a formal examination, there is only one answer which examiners can accept; therefore the success of each 'student' translator can be measured according to previously-agreed criteria. Difference of quality will emerge in the understanding and recreation of nuance and idiom, but basically the translation is either correct or not and therefore an identical approach can be adopted in estimating the success of each student.

If, however, each participant is learning something different, as happens in experiential activities when they are encouraged to develop their own learning cycles even in the same exercise, this kind of measurement is impossible. In the example given above of an exercise designed to enhance the understanding of leadership, one participant will identify the inappropriateness of the leadership adopted during the *Do* part of this particular session. A second may have realised that during the course of the activity a whole range of different leadership styles was apparent and will be evaluating the best way to employ them, and a third could be trying to understand the unofficial leadership which was being exercised by another member of the group. Each personally will have achieved some significant learning, but each piece of learning is different in quality and depth. No common measurement of success is possible.

Third, what the tutor hopes will be the learning from an activity, and what the students actually find they have learned, may be totally different. It was noted in Chapter 7 how two exercises (Water Bomb 2 and Triple Crown) designed by a tutor to provide learning about matching skills to job requirements had from the tutors' perspective achieved little. However, the students had clearly achieved substantial learning in the field of group work and from their point of view it was a success. By no stretch of the imagination was the exercise a failure, but any gain for the students was at the expense of the objectives originally sought by that tutor.

Finally, in experiential learning success will come for different students at different speeds and at different times. In transmissive learning student achievements can be tested, if required, at a specific time on a specific date. That is when the examination or interview will take place, when the essay or thesis must be complete or when the demonstration will occur. If we return again to the example of the experiential activity designed to provide learning about the skills of leadership, one participant may have the opportunity of demonstrating the success of the process within a matter of minutes. For another it may be a matter of days or even weeks before any learning has been absorbed and the student has the opportunity and the confidence to put the new skills or knowledge into practice. It would be both pointless and unrealistic to attempt to evaluate the success for each participant at the same time.

Means of evaluation

The fact that evaluation of the success of experiential learning is different to that of transmissive learning and that it is complicated by the factors described above does not mean that no evaluation should be attempted. Even though no common or traditionally quantifiable measurement is possible, it would be irresponsible not to attempt to evaluate whether experiential learning is proving successful. Without such efforts it will be impossible to justify time given to experiential learning or to persuade those who know nothing of it to commit themselves to it. If they did not attempt to evaluate, tutors would be abdicating a key responsibility. Experiential learning thrives on the notion of encouraging students to control their own learning, but the accountability of tutors still continues.

Where and how, then, does this evaluation take place? Given that it is in the *Review* that the majority of learning opportunities emerge, to be followed up subsequently by the tutor, it is clearly necessary to have some criteria by which to judge whether the *Review* has been successful for some or all of the participants. However, it is not only the *Review* which is important; it depends at least in part on a successful *Do*.

If the activity or exercise has failed to rouse the interest and imagination of the students, if they have found it irrelevant or inappropriate to their needs or intellectual level, then the *Review* will suffer accordingly. Indeed the students' opportunity for learning may be limited to discovering what it was that made the activity unpalatable to them and how they felt about and reacted to this. So there need to be criteria also for evaluating the success or otherwise of the activity – the *Do*. If both the *Do* and the *Review* have been successful, then the tutor can be satisfied that a good basis for assisting students to construct their own learning cycle has been provided.

What makes a good Do?

A successful experiential activity, either indoors or outdoors, will depend initially on its ability to capture the interest and imagination of the participants, and subsequently on its providing the appropriate intellectual and/or physical challenge to maintain this interest. It must, therefore, in the first instance appeal to the spirit of adventure, intellect, imagination or sense of humour of as many of the students as possible. An invitation to tackle some of the physical activities described in Chapter 9 may well do this, as may an analytical problem to solve (particularly for those of greater academic ability) or something which makes them laugh. *Darlington Station* – an exercise designed to encourage learning about problem solving in groups starts with the preamble 'Darlington Football Club has been drawn to play Liverpool in the semi-final of the F A Cup' and has shown that it can gain the initial interest and commitment of the students simply through the unlikely, almost ludicrous, nature of its premise.

Having gained the commitment of the participants, a successful experiential activity will need to provide continuing stimulation and enjoyment at the appropriate intellectual level. Anything too simple runs the risk of being dismissed as unworthy of serious intellectual effort; anything too complex quickly fosters discouragement and disillusionment. Although learning may still be gained in both these situations, it stands to be diminished as the main purpose of the activity will have been negated.

Other crucial factors in maintaining interest and commitment are accuracy of timing and suitability of environment. The exercise must have about it sufficient urgency to compel continuing intellectual and/or physical activity on the part of the participants, but not such urgency as to make the task impossible or to prevent a suitably thoughtful and planned approach to it. Conversely there must not be so much time available that impetus is lost and complacency or, worse than that, boredom ensues. In the best exercises most students, if not all, perceive a purposefulness relative to their own needs.

Equally, the physical environment for the exercise must be such that it allows the participants the best possible opportunity of operating without unnecessary distraction and with appropriate comfort and convenience. A very small group in a very large room (or vice versa), unnecessarily noisy surroundings when concentration is called for, hostile weather conditions in outdoor activity and demands beyond the requirements of the exercise or the competence of the participants are all examples of situations where success is jeopardised by an unsuitable environment.

Finally, the activity must be guided with tutorship that, as far as possible, is non-directive. Instructions need to be clear and unambiguous (unless the solution of ambiguity is one of the aims of the exercise), and tutors must have sufficient knowledge of, and confidence in, their materials to refrain from intrusion into the activity, only to respond to queries when invited (and only then to respond within the parameters of the exercise), and not to intervene except in case of emergency. All this presupposes a high level of planning and a deal of experience as outlined in previous chapters.

A successful Do – a checklist

Given the criteria for a successful experiential activity described above, tutors can best assess the success or otherwise of any particular exercise or *Do* component by seeking the answers to the following questions. They ought to remember, though, that their estimates and those of individual participants will not necessarily be the same and that each person's perception of success is equally valid. However, it is reasonable to assume that if the consensus of those taking part is favourable, tutors have on this occasion and with this exercise achieved success.

1 Was the idea behind the exercise immediately attractive?
2 Did the exercise maintain interest as it progressed?
3 Was the exercise sufficiently challenging intellectually?
4 Did most students regard their activity as purposeful?
5 Was the exercise in any way unreasonably demanding?
6 Did all students appear to become involved in the exercise?
7 Was the briefing/instructions for the exercise sufficiently clear?
8 Was the environment for the exercise suitable?
9 Were the resources for the exercise adequate?
10 Was the time allowed for the exercise reasonable?
11 Did some groups (or individual students) finish early, or not have time to complete?
12 Did my role as tutor become over-directive?
13 Was this because I chose it to be so, or through some inadequacy in planning?
14 Did it seem that I failed to give adequate guidance?
15 Did the students appear to look forward to the *Review*?

What makes a good Review?

maximum benefit in learning, and where opportunities for follow-up present themselves to the tutor. The starting point, therefore, for most students is an exercise which they have found interesting and 'appropriate' to their expectations. Tutors will hope also that some opportunities for learning are available to them, as they guide their students from the *Do* stage into *Review*.

What, then, are the criteria necessary for a supportive learning environment during the *Review* stage? First, there must be a subtle combination of spontaneity and direction. The atmosphere must be such that during the *Review* students are able to talk about their experiences and feelings of whatever kind without being inhibited by restrictive tutorship or unhelpful behaviour from fellow students. What tutors intend or imagine will emerge during the *Review* of a particular exercise may well not, even though it has regularly done so on previous occasions.

For their own part tutors should not be so concerned about their own perceptions of the likely learning that they prevent other insights and feelings from emerging. However, this does not mean that no guidance is necessary. A totally unstructured *Review* can be as frustrating to students as one which is over-directed. It is a very narrow tightrope which tutors have to walk to achieve this fine balance between spontaneity on the part of the students and the imposition of guidance and structure.

Second, the atmosphere must be such that real openness will be possible, and in this context tutors must assume a large measure of responsibility. This openness will take two forms. There will be the freedom for all members of the group to describe their perceptions, reactions and emotions, knowing that they can rely on the support and understanding of other group members. There will also be the freedom to give and receive feed-back without causing either offence or embarrassment. Often this can happen in sub-groups as a few students consider how they completed a task before taking part in a wider discussion with the whole group.

It must be open to all participants to ask for reactions to their own behaviour and to state how other participants have helped or hindered their learning. Tutors need to work towards situations in which criticism can be accepted without rancour and praise without disclaimer. This atmosphere will not, of course, be there on the first occasion on which a group meets, but it will grow with familiarity, especially if the tutor has the expertise and experience to create the atmosphere which will foster it. Sometimes, though, tutors will find it difficult to cultivate such an ambience either because of the behaviour of one or two students, or on account of not wanting to appear over-intrusive. Inter-personal and inter-group relationships have to be allowed to develop, on occasion, without the intervention of the tutor.

Third, as with a good *Do*, the physical environment of the *Review* is crucial. The room, the availability of time and the organisational arrangements provided by the tutor can all contribute to an appropriate environment. Such matters once again come back to the tutor. Perhaps the most straightforward way of describing the tutor skills required during the *Review* stage is in terms of purposefulness. Tutors must not be over-intrusive; they have to allow group processes to develop, but they must ensure that as many students as possible regard the *Review* as purposeful, both as a follow-up to the *Do* stage and in relation to what they expect to learn from the session.

There are no easy answers about how tutors may achieve this state of affairs, but one reasonable approach they can adopt is to try to place themselves on the side of students – for it is their interests which ought to dominate the *Review*. The following series of questions, posed from a student's perspective, should help tutors think through with students the relative success of a *Review*.

A successful Review – a checklist

1 Was I able to express my views openly?
2 Did others listen when I was speaking?
3 Did I listen when others were speaking?
4 Did I have the confidence to give feed-back honestly?
5 Was I able to receive praise without demur?
6 Was I able to receive unpalatable feed-back without negative reaction?
7 Did the tutor help members of the group to express and share their views and feelings?
8 Were the interventions of the tutor helpful?
9 Was the role of the tutor over-directive?
10 Was the environment suitable for the Review?
11 Was sufficient time allowed for the Review?
12 Was the tutor able to follow through some of the points which emerged?
13 Were there opportunities for the tutor to relate events to real-life situations?
14 Did the tutor attempt any generalisations?
15 Did I find these useful?
16 Were they relevant to my needs?
17 Did I discover things I did not know as a result of the Review?

'Triumphs' – three examples of good practice

It might be helpful at this point to cite three examples of exercises which have in the past proved successful on a number of occasions in both the

Do and the *Review* stage. They are essentially very different, and all are included in the Exercise Section.

1 Indivisible Load

Indivisible Load was written by Tony Brennan during the late 1960s when he was a Training Officer with ICI, and it has been widely used and adapted by others since.

Essentially, *Indivisible Load* was produced as a problem-solving exercise. It has been found to have a high degree of success as an 'ice-breaker' – an activity to start a course or introduce a group to experiential learning. It is also a useful medium for learning about group skills, and has proved valuable in this context in assisting work groups (senior management teams in schools, for example) to reflect upon their working practices and procedures, as part of a team-building process.

The strategem in this exercise is to give each member of the group slightly different but, in most respects, visually identical information. This opens up the whole area of communication; most particularly the way in which every individual brings to any problem different knowledge and information, either technical and explicit or based on experiences and implicit. If a member of the team is designated leader, issues related to leadership and the willingness of other team members to follow or ignore the leads that are given can be emphasised.

The nature of the problem has generally been found intriguing and challenging. It leads almost invariably to lively activity, in which all group members must participate if 'their team' is to be successful. An element of competition between the teams can be introduced, and the *Review* usually raises a number of interesting issues which depend upon the emphasis the tutor has given to the exercise. Most students seem to appreciate the learning *Indivisible Load* offers them, whether it be about group processes, leadership or communication skills. The exercise has proved suitable for participants of all ages.

2 Darlington Station

Another exercise devised by Tony Brennan is called Darlington Station (for obvious reasons). It has some similarities to *Indivisible Load* but tends to produce different behaviour patterns. Although not suitable as an ice-breaker, it can be used to promote communication skills and studies of group work.

3 Appraisal

The third exercise – *Appraisal* – is quite different. It was devised by Chris Parkin, a Training Manager at Rowntree, to use with a group of senior and experienced teachers who were approaching the problem of introducing appraisal to the staff of a secondary school for the first time. It was designed as an activity which would be totally divorced from the school scene but which would give participants the feeling of appraising and being appraised in a real and relevant part of their everyday lives. As an exercise it demands a substantial amount of time and has proved disappointing when this was not available and it had to be hurried. It is an extremely good example of how an experiential activity blends naturally into transmissive learning, and how both styles are important and can, when used skilfully, be complementary.

Appraisal is becoming increasingly common both in business and in other professions such as teaching. Appraisal is one of those activities which, if done badly, may not only be ineffective but can also be demotivating and potentially damaging.

Appraisal raises difficult problems, and is always more complex than it seems at first. The issues involved initially seem to be fairly clear (about being frank with people, telling them where they did not do well and helping them improve). However, on closer examination, appraisal is also about the appraiser, about the organisation (the school or company in which the appraisee operates) and the forces which help him or her to be effective or ineffective. It is about perception of roles, about self-confidence, about willingness and ability to change, about training and coaching and practise and above all about self-improvement. It is also about everyday improvement over a period and is not simply about the appraisal 'interview'. The interview is a means to an end and not an end in itself – although it appears to be an end in itself to many people.

The choice in appraisal training is usually between role-playing (using a prepared brief, acting the parts, and trying to stay within the brief yet conduct a dynamic discussion) or using a classroom task as the content which often feels trivial and also 'artificial'. The activity described on page 197 of the Exercise Section attempts to limit the role-playing restrictions and increase the 'real' feelings.

Disasters

Throughout this book the reader will have been able to identify the wide range of skills, experience and resources which are needed if experiential learning is to be successful. It goes without saying that if these skills, experience and resources are missing, failure – either partial or total – is likely to follow. It would be tedious to list all the things that can go wrong, as most of them will have become obvious to the reader already, but a summary of the most blatant examples may be helpful.

It is a sobering thought that most disasters are tutor-made. True, there are students who can destroy experiential learning either deliberately or accidentally, but even here the blame can normally be laid on the tutor either because of thoughtless planning, which has indicated or permitted the disruption, or through lack of skill in handling it when it occurs. Most disasters can in fact be attributed directly either to a tutor's lack of planning or to limitations in skill and/or experience.

Inadequacies in planning

Bad planning lies mainly in two categories. One is in the choice of material to be used in experiential activity. If the chosen exercise is at the wrong intellectual level, failure is predictable. Something that is too simple is boring; something too complex is frustrating. There can be an element of luck in this if the tutor has not met a group before, or if it contains a wide range of abilities, but often selection of the wrong material is a sign of slipshod preparation.

Likewise if the exercise is simply repeating something done previously with no natural progression, or has been put into the programme without any real purpose other than to plug a gap, failure is likely. The temptation to use experiential activity as a game – 'Now for something completely different' – must be avoided at all costs. Inexperienced tutors may be tempted to stop at the *Do* stage; they may lack the confidence to proceed to *Review*. However, only if the *Do* and *Review* are completed do individual students have the opportunity to move on to complete their learning cycles.

The other category of bad planning, as described earlier, comes about through lack of proper attention to the environment of the activity. If instruction sheets are insufficient, inaccurate or need updating; if the room is inadequate in size, or furnishing; if essential equipment or resources are missing or incomplete; or if the time allowed for the exercise is inappropriate, the atmosphere conducive to the most productive learning will be destroyed.

Sometimes the activity may falter altogether, where the unsuitability of the environment and the inadequacy of the resources prevent it continuing. When this occurs, even the most confident and experienced of tutors will find it difficult to extract any learning from such a situation. Opportunities for learning do arise when sessions proceed in ways a tutor has not intended, perhaps because some students are reluctant to become involved in an activity or its *Review*, for such situations can be exploited by tutors. However, when they arise through inadequate planning, and this is obvious to students, not only do tutors stand to lose credibility – so too does the whole notion of experiential learning.

Lack of skill and expertise

Bad planning is one of the two major causes of disasters. Bad tutorship is the other. If possible, all potential tutors need the opportunity to work, in the first instance, in a team along with others with more experience – from whom they can learn skills and with whom they can gain confidence.

It is also essential that inexperienced tutors, in particular, examine all material extremely carefully before using it, trying to identify possible pitfalls and how these may be confronted. Many published materials do in fact include guidance as to the degree of tutor skill needed to use them.

Inexperienced or unskilled tutorship manifests itself most commonly in such things as an inappropriate style (over-directive, condescending, flippant etc); poor timing – especially underestimating time requirements; rushing the *Review* and any follow-up teaching while pre-empting possible silences from the students; a lack of empathy with the participants, especially those who may be having difficulty in contributing or expressing their feelings; and an inability to handle difficult situations sensitively.

From time to time students will express anger or frustration, will become destructively dominant or relapse into silence, will try (for whatever reason) to provoke the tutor, or will expose more of their sensitive feelings than they intended and wish to escape from the position in which they now find themselves. In situations such as these the skill and experience of the tutor are vital. Tutors should not embark on exercises in which such behaviour is likely to emerge unless they have the confidence that they can handle such complex and sensitive inter-personal behaviour.

'Murphy's Law'

Even if planning has been exemplary and skill and experience are entirely appropriate for the activity, disaster can still be snatched from the jaws of victory. This can easily come about from some totally unexpected and unpredictable circumstances and, of course, in experiential learning, as opposed to more transmissive styles of teaching, once the thread is broken, it is seldom possible to put it together again. In the authors' experience, such operations of Murphy's Law have included unexpected fire alarms, alteration in a programme resulting in the halving of available time, key group members being called away for family crises, and the non-appearance, without notice, of half or more of the anticipated membership of an experiential learning session. On one occasion, a visiting Inspector asked to be allowed to attend a session in which groups of sixth formers were engaged in a complex problem-solving exercise against the clock. He proceeded to join each group in turn to discuss not the exercise but individual career intentions of group members. Not surprisingly, this Inspector has not been invited subsequently!

New tutors will be relieved to know that such occurrences are not all that frequent and that no tutor, however skilful or experienced, could easily achieve a triumph under some of the adverse circumstances of this type that have occurred. Schools and colleges are busy and complex organisations, and unanticipated disturbances are quite unavoidable on many occasions.

11 Return to reality

The meaning of reality

No style of learning will gain credibility unless it is seen by students to be applicable to reality. One of the criticisms of experiential learning has been that it too often becomes 'game playing', that no real learning takes place because nothing has been gained which can be used outside the class or lecture-room. Our submission is that when experiential learning is described in this way it is either a very poor example of the style, which perhaps concentrates too much on a *Do* to the exclusion of *Review*, or is no more than a 'filler' because a tutor cannot think of anything more appropriate.

Sometimes critics of experiential learning confuse it with role play or simulation. In some situations these activities prove highly appropriate learning approaches, but they differ markedly from experiential learning.

There is a real danger that these latter styles of learning depart from reality in that participants are positively encouraged either to *act* a role or to simulate a person or a personality which is not their own. They are encouraged to adopt behaviour which is unreal.

For any learning to have been real, two things must have happened. First the students must be able to identify specific things learned either about the subject being studied (delegation, leadership, communication or whatever) or about themselves, their strengths and weaknesses. Second, they must see a way or ways in which the learning can be applied to improve or modify what they may be called upon to do in the future. If these two elements are missing, as is possible in role play and simulation, then real learning has not occurred. It is possible to explore this concept further by considering one experiential exercise in which there is a real danger that role play or simulation will take over unless care is exercised.

Capitation Committee, an exercise designed by Kirk (1987, pp. 143–146), has the stated objectives of improving the negotiating, influencing and consensus skills of participants. It involves five 'briefing sheets', each of which describes the situation in a secondary school department when a tranche of money is made available for curriculum development. Five students are given a briefing sheet each and asked to represent a department at a meeting which is to decide the distribution of this extra money. Their task is completed when the money is allocated. The problem is that the claims of the departments exceed the money available, and the members must argue for their 'share' of the money with the information they possess about departmental needs.

If the group is to complete its task then members must negotiate, so that initial claims can be scaled down or priorities are determined which may involve depriving some departments altogether. They must (and they do) try to influence one another, by forming alliances and sometimes by attempting to discredit the arguments of other group members who they regard as competitors. When agreement is reached it will represent some sort of consensus. The opportunities that a tutor can bring out during *Review* are wide-ranging. The meaning of the term consensus, for example, can be considered. Were all members satisfied with the outcome? The actual processes of negotiating and influencing which emerged as the group moved towards an allocation of the money can be studied. The behaviour of group members can be reported by an observer, and many inter-personal and inter-group attributes can be debated.

In terms of promoting learning, the key issue of which a tutor needs to be aware is that although the situation is artificial, the processes occurring in the *Do* and the topics discussed in the *Review* relate closely to reality. The way in which group members negotiate, influence and accept consensus are not likely to be very different from those adopted in other situations, wholly divorced from a school capitation committee. A student at the 'wrong end' of an imposed consensus, whose behaviour is noted by an observer, may act very differently in future. Similarly, someone whose over-bearing behaviour alienates others to the point of receiving no allocation will have received useful feedback for future occasions.

Then there is the question of how best to make a decision in these circumstances. The arrangement which members must follow on this occasion is that the group decides. Each member has information about their department, and therefore possesses expert knowledge. The position of the expert can therefore be introduced into the *Review*, as can the necessity of checking what the expect says (but how can you do this, not in the exercise, but in real life?). If a chairperson is designated, this role can be considered. The notion of a neutral chairperson often comes in for criticism, usually within more general discussion of the most appropriate way in which the decisions should be made, both in this example and in other situations where there are too many claims on too few resources.

The exercise is not a simulation. The intention is not to replicate a school resource committee. This point is sometimes misunderstood, even by potential tutors. As the stated objectives try to make clear, the exercise can be an opportunity to consider various aspects of individual and group behaviour when a decision must be made. Therefore it can be, and has been, used with students from many different backgrounds. Indeed, only when the students are teachers, and more particularly senior staff, does the simulation issue arise. Such participants sometimes become too concerned with questions which are unimportant in the context of the exercise – Why are only five departments represented? Why is the headteacher absent? Why does the briefing sheet not provide more information etc. They appear to think the objective is to study how an equivalent committee would function in a school.

Learning may, of course, result when teachers perceive the exercise as simulation. It is not uncommon for less senior staff who want more openness in their school to realise the problems of a forum of specialist interests arriving at a consensus. Many are tempted to suggest that the head should continue to decide, but the disadvantages of that approach need to be raised by the tutor. However, if staff do regard *Capitation Committee* as simulation then the other objectives relating to negotiation, influencing and consensus skills of students, and issues relating to teamwork and group decision-making, may receive too little attention.

Capitation Committee is not a role-play exercise. Students are not asked to play the role of the head of department, but to represent the department at a meeting. Therefore, prior student knowledge is of no real significance. Secondary school teachers in particular sometimes object to criticisms that a student who teaches Science cannot represent the Business Studies department, because it is assumed that a Business Studies teacher will be the best at 'acting' the part of the head of depart-ment. A tutor may need to guide students away from this thinking, and introduce it as a topic in the *Review*, if appropriate. With steady guidance, though, an experienced tutor can move students away from a simulation or role-play attitude towards the many objectives which this particular exercise can help achieve. A revised version of *Capitation Committee* is included on page 161 in the Exercise Section.

Experiential learning as natural learning

Capitation Committee is a good example of how organised experiential learning can extend and accelerate the natural learning of students – that which occurs as a result of students' everyday experiences. Learning cycles are being constructed most of the time by all of us, because of what we do, read, see and as a result of what happens. Usually, this occurs unsystematically and without too much overt awareness.

It would be an odd student who joined a session without any skills in negotiating, influencing and consensus forming, who knew nothing about groups and how they perform. However, for most students much of what has been learned has come from natural experience, aided by advice (often unsolicited) from family, friends and colleagues. Participation in *Capitation Committee* should refine and concentrate these processes of natural learning. Students are offered a particular experience – taking part in a group which is making a choice. They will have been involved in this type of activity on numerous previous occasions. On this occasion the outcome does not really matter, but the nature of their participation may have been observed so that they receive objective feedback. As a result students will be able to join a discussion in which other students discuss what they did, they will be able to check how decisions related to behaviour and they will have opportunities to consider their own feelings compared with those of fellow students.

Of course, not every student will be able to realise the learning opportunities that arise from an activity like *Capitation Committee* on every occasion. This book has tried to analyse the problems of tutors and, as a result, has considered many ways in which exercises can go wrong, so that the *Review* and any subsequent follow-up (if attempted) are of no avail. The *Do* may become a role-play, so that a student can discuss some constructive comment about behaviour as a result of acting.

Some students may try to disrupt the session for a variety of reasons, others may not wish to exercise their skills in negotiating or influencing, possibly because they feel sufficiently confident with their present levels or, more likely, because they do not want to risk appearing deficient in front of colleagues or classmates. Such attitudes are understandable and require careful handling by tutors. Natural learning, by its very definition, occurs all the time in normal surroundings. Students generally control their own learning processes without interference, and can avoid any embarrassment of not learning by withdrawing.

Such withdrawals are possible (and should not be hindered by tutors) during experiential sessions but they become more public in this context.

Sometimes they are physical (a student leaves the group); more often (and more threateningly to a tutor) they involve a lack of response or commitment. Usually the excuse offered by students is that the whole activity is unrealistic – it does not relate to anything they do or are likely to do outside.

More obliquely, such students are saying that the experiential education organised for them fails to extend their natural learning, or seems likely to take it in directions they would not approve. Yet to be able to make such a choice represents a good deal of progress. It means that students have become more aware of their own natural learning processes, and the extent to which these can be extended and accelerated by tutor-organised sessions.

Areas of proven worth

To many people experiential learning still sounds like something new and experimental, something to approach with caution. It may, therefore, be helpful to indicate a number of areas where such learning is generally accepted in school and college programmes.

1 GCSE

The introducton of GCSE provided an impetus to learning of an experiential nature. Fieldwork, problem solving and skill-based learning, if properly handled, can all contribute to the process of learning through activity and *Review*. GCSE is the culmination of a process which has been natural in primary education for many years, which now has been extended to many junior forms in secondary education, and which developed through aspects of CSE and through the 16+ examination.

If one looks at typical examples of work in Technology, we find that it is now normal practice to start learning by posing a problem for students to experiment with and design their own solutions. No preliminary 'instruction' is given, and students work out basic principles for resolving the problem which can subsequently be applied to comparable situations.

For instance, the introductory module for a fourth year GCSE group might be a photograph showing an elderly person trying to negotiate a wheelchair through a pair of swing doors at the head of a short flight of steps. Students have to identify the precise nature of the problems and suggest solutions. Quite obviously such a situation contains sufficient variables to ensure that a range of solutions will emerge. Alternatively the problem may consist of a simple design brief to which students have to respond by building their own model (see example below). In both cases the essential feature is that the learning cycle: *Do – Review – Learn – Apply* must be followed.

Situation

A building site is operating in your area. The builders are working on two levels above the ground and are constantly having to climb down to ground level to collect materials such as bricks and mortar.

Design brief/specification

Design and build a model hoist system capable of lifting loads of up to 10N (1kg) to two different levels. The hoist must not operate if the load exceeds

10N and/or the safety cage on the hoist platform is not closed. Once started the hoist should stop automatically at the first level, remain there for 30 seconds, and then continue on to level two where it should stop once more.

2 Personal and Social Education and Religious Education

PSE and Religious Education are other areas which lend themselves readily to experiential learning. Many of the materials suggested in Chapter 6 help participants to involve themselves in moral or ethical issues, engage the emotions and, at the *Review* stage, require the sharing of prejudices and values. Such exercises are challenging, open-ended and full of opportunity for learning which can be applied to other situations.

One such exercise requires the group members to discuss the respective claims and merits of five patients who are in need of a kidney transplant. Only one kidney is available and therefore it must be assumed that the four patients whose case is rejected are unlikely to survive. The only criterion provided is that the prognosis for people over 40 years of age who receive a transplant kidney is less hopeful than for those under 40. The group is required to reach a consensus.

The five candidates are: a 42-year-old married man with two teenage children who is engaged on research into a cancer immunisation drug; a 27-year-old black vehicle fitter, married with a three-year-old daughter and another baby on the way; a 30-year-old housewife, married to a self-employed accountant, with five children aged from 10 to four months; a 19-year-old male undergraduate who is engaged to be married and hoping tc become a university lecturer, and a marketing manager in a large manufacturing organisation who is an unmarried woman of 34. The group is also given some further information about the interests and personality of each of the candidates. For instance, the undergraduate is bright with a lot of good prospects for the future, but at the same time much involved as a student activist. He is almost paranoid about his ill-ess. The housewife is deeply religious and described as a professional 'do gooder'. The scientist is on the verge of an important breakthrough in his work, but his commitment to his research has put his family relations under strain.

As will easily be seen, discussion within the group will soon cause individual beliefs and values to emerge. Feelings will be affected, even passions aroused, as the group attempts to establish priorities and achieve consensus. The *Review* provides the opportunity for members to examine their own behaviour and value systems, and to learn more about themselves. This enhanced personal understanding ought to be applicable to further situations and should help in the development of mature and balanced judgements.

3 Careers Education

Experiential learning is common in Careers Education and can be used in a number of different ways. First, there is a variety of exercises suitable for self-assessment. Individuals can use these to identify their own strengths and weaknesses and to identify their suitability or potential for different areas of employment. Similarly, there are exercises for groups to explore the same themes. *Water Bomb 1* and *Water Bomb 2* (see Chapter 7) are examples of these two types of exercise. Such exercises add variety to the more transmissive mode of Careers Education where the nature and requirements of various job families are examined.

In addition Careers Education lends itself to a number of practical activities, which, if they are presented and reviewed fully, are highly experiential. Interview schemes and work experience are two examples of these. Students can be encouraged to discuss what they have gained from such activities, the extent to which their expectations were met, and their likely response to further similar experiences. It must, however, be emphasised that a proper introduction before the external experience, and a skilfully-organised *Review*, are essential. Students must be encouraged to think through and analyse their experiences, to assess their achievement and/or failures and to apply this learning to future events.

4 Economic Awareness, Business Education, Enterprise

The range of practical activities in Economic Awareness and, more particularly, Business Education and Enterprise, from which experiential learning can arise, is extensive and obvious. For Economic Awareness the Economic Awareness Teacher Training programme (ECATT) has devised a number of experiential exercises from which participants may learn to ask appropriate questions, and to decide priorities based on values which have been established and clarified during the activity. Some of these exercises are similar in style, purpose, flexibility and application to the *World Trade Game* discussed in Chapter 8.

Business Education and Enterprise include a number of opportunities for students to become involved in real activities from which learning will emerge, sometimes in painful and surprising ways. An enterprise scheme does not have to include making a profit (in fact some of the best ones do not), but on one occasion in which it did, the manager of a 6th form company designing and making fencing for use in the school grounds found that he did not have the skill or equipment to cut a particular shape of timber. He asked a member of staff for help, and was amazed the next day to receive a bill for the teacher's time and services. The learning he gained in this unfortunate way (his company nearly went bankrupt) may well be applied to future situations in his career. Another student representing a different 6th form company signed a contract with the head for use of the school's facilities to run a lunchtime video club, only to discover that she had not read the small print and that almost her entire potential profit was mortgaged. Here was the truth of the saying, 'there are two ways of gaining experience – by doing and by being done'!

5 CPVE and TVEI

CPVE and TVEI, while two very different initiatives, are similar in that both have a strong pre-vocational element and contain an emphasis on self-evaluation. The latter is accentuated in the case of TVEI by the recent introduction of Records of Achievement. We have already seen in the section on Careers Education how meaningful experiential learning can be both in pre-vocational activities and in identifying personal strengths, weaknesses and potential.

The core element of CPVE also contains extensive requirements in the areas of communication, problem solving and working in groups. Experiential activity is now commonplace in all these areas of learning, and the reader will have noticed how often they have been referred to in previous chapters.

Staff development

Experiential activity is an accepted means of learning for all ages. The techniques are the same whatever the age and experience of the participants, and the majority of materials can be used at any level. The depth of the learning will vary, the medium is constant.

One unexpected 'spin-off' has been the way in which staff have applied the methods used in their own learning to work with pupils. Part of the learning process has been the realisation that the experiential methods used have been so powerful that it is only natural to use them with students also. There have been interesting variants to this as well.

One head attended a course on interviewing run by a local firm for its middle management. Most of the learning was by experiential methods and great emphasis was laid on the techniques of asking questions correctly. Young people from a local technical college acted as interviewees (experiential learning for them also) and a careful check was kept that the interviewer's questions were open-ended and provided the candidates with the maximum space in which to describe their qualifications, experience, aspirations, interests and so on. The head found not only that the course transformed his subsequent interviewing of candidates for posts at the school, but even more so that it had a profound influence on his teaching. The skill of asking open-ended questions had become so much a part of his natural style that he was bringing far more out of his pupils in class. The application of what he had learned could be transferred easily and naturally to a different area of his professional life.

Some potential inhibitors

Despite the obvious importance and value of experiential methods as a means of learning, there are a number of factors at work on the educational scene at present which may inhibit its further development. The first is the introduction of the National Curriculum. The problem here is that curricular emphasis is exclusively on content. Admittedly there is no statement as to how the curriculum is to be taught, but the fact that the levels of attainment required are described and that the means of assessment are laid down must militate against an experiential, process-based method of learning.

In subjects where the transmissive mode is appropriate for some or all of the learning this will not be serious. In others, however, the loss of experiential activity could seriously detract from the quality of the learning on offer. It is of particular concern that in the Whole Curriculum, of which the National Curriculum is part, Personal and Social Education is itemised under five headings – Economic Awareness, Health Education, Careers, Environmental Education and Citizenship. Not only are various elements omitted altogether (for example, social skills across the total range), but the fact that these items are all part of a whole developmental process is ignored. Good schools will certainly try to retain what they already offer successfully, but the pressure of a crowded timetable and perhaps of contrary demands on the part of parents and governors may be difficult to resist.

The way ahead: future developments

In time perhaps the most valuable feature that will emerge from Baker Days and the increased emphasis on in-service training, is that for five working days per year (at least) teachers once again become students. They are supposed to learn new skills, knowledge and understanding. They are exposed to many forms of teaching, and as a result they are likely to become more aware of their own learning requirements and how these interact with in-service sessions in which they become involved. On some topics they may prefer a didactic approach, on others they will appreciate an experiential model, when they have the opportunity to

'Do', take part in a *Review* and have their perceptions heightened by a tutor's insights and theoretical perspectives.

As has already been noted, staff returning from management courses, which often adopt an experiential approach, have been more willing to experiment with experiential exercises. They have learned that a variety of approaches is best. The main problem for tutors is first to have the confidence to use such a variety and second to possess the skill, gained from experience, to determine which is the most appropriate approach given the student group, its background, previous experiences and the environment of the sessions (timing, room, availability of materials etc).

The aim of this book is not to demonstrate experiential learning as the answer to all institutionalised teaching and learning problems. A particular form of experiential learning has been discussed, and the advantages and disadvantages associated with it considered. Other approaches to learning have been somewhat downgraded by comparison but that is not to say that they do not have a perfectly legitimate role in the techniques adopted by a competent tutor. Indeed, a more didactic approach to teaching is likely to prevail for the foreseeable future.

Ideally all tutors would possess a range of approaches, in which the *Do – Review – Learn – Apply* sequence of experiential learning is highly significant. This book has tried to explain why it is so significant and what can be gained by teachers using the approach in a wide range of situations. The focus has been on tutors who use the experiential mode, those who wonder whether they should adopt it, and those who feel themselves being forced into experimenting with what, for them, will be an untried and, perhaps, threatening situation. In all cases, the intention has been to offer encouragement, guidance and ideas so that both tutors and students can gain from the many attractive features of the *Do – Review – Learn – Apply* approach to experiential learning.

Bibliography

Argyris, C. (1982) *Reasoning, Learning and Action: Individual and Organisation*. Jossey Bass.

Bloom, B.S. (1964) *Taxonomy of Educational Objectives: The Classification of Educational Goals. Handbooks I & II*. Longman.

Brandes, D. and Ginnis, P. (1986) *A Guide to Student-Centred Learning*. Basil Blackwell.

Brandes, D. and Phillips, H. (1980) *The Gamesters' Handbook: 140 games for teachers and group leaders*. Hutchinson Education.

Bruner, J.S. (1971) *Toward a Theory of Instruction*. Harvard University Press.

Dennison, W.F. and Shenton, K. (1987) *Challenges in Educational Management: Principles into Practice*. Croom Helm.

Dubin, P. (1962) *Human Relations in Administration*. Prentice-Hall.

Further Education Curriculum Review and Development Unit (1977) *Experience, Reflection, Learning*.

Honey, P. (1984) 'Building on Learning Styles'. *Training and Development*.

Honey, P. and Mumford, A. (1982) *Using your Learning Styles*. Honey.

Kirk, R.F. (1987) *Learning in Action*. Basil Blackwell.

Knowles, M.S. (1984) *Andragogy in Action*. McGraw-Hill.

Kolb, D.A. (1983) *Experiential Learning: Experience as the Source of Learning and Development*. Prentice-Hall.

Luft, J. (1970) 'Johari's Window: An experience in self-disclosure and feedback' *in* Pfeiffer, J.W. and Jones, J.E. (eds) *A handbook of structured experience for human relations training*. University Associates.

Maslow, A.H. (1959) *Motivation and Personality*. Harper.

Mumford, A. (1982) 'Learning Styles and Learning Skills'. *Journal of Management Development* Vol.1, No.2.

Mumford, A. (1984) 'Effectiveness in Management Development'. *Journal of Management Development* Vol.3, No. 2.

Putnam, R. (1988) *A Rationale for Outward Bound*. Outward Bound Trust.

Revans, R.W. (1980) *Learning in Action*. Blond and Briggs.

Schon, D.A. (1987) *Educating the Reflective Practitioner: Toward a New Design for Teaching and Learning*. Jossey-Bass.

Part 3

The Exercises

The exercises in this section are presented in a variety of styles. The reason for this is twofold: first, the exercises vary widely in content and approach; second, it is intended that this variety will promote flexibility in their use.

WATER BOMB 1

An earlier version of this exercise appears on p 85 in Chapter 7.

Objectives	• to help participants realise the importance of a realistic assessment of their skills, capabilities and experience
	• to stimulate thinking about the matching of these skills, capabilities and experience to real jobs and career planning
Description	Individuals in competition are asked to calculate how many water bombs they can make in 20 minutes. They then make the bombs and compare the outcome with their forecasts.
Target group	Years 4–5, 6th form, staff
Organisation	One tutor per 15 participants plus observers
Time required	1 hour. This can be extended with a longer *Review*.
Tutor skills	This exercise can be tackled by tutors with little previous experience.
Location	Any room large enough to give the individuals adequate working space.
Materials	One briefing sheet per participant
	One *Water Bomb* construction sheet per participant
	Paper for construction (A4 size tests manipulative skills; larger will test use of space)

Tutor's notes

1 Issue each participant with a briefing sheet and a *Water Bomb* construction sheet. Remind them that they have 10 minutes for planning. State the quality of construction you will expect. Give them any instructions you think necessary about timing (the dynamics can be noticeably different if you time them, if they time themselves, or if nothing is said about timing at all). (*15 minutes*)

2 Collect in declaration tear-off strips. Dispose of all trial bombs. Issue paper. Announce start of construction time. (*5 minutes*)

3 Participants work on task. (*20 minutes*)

4 Task ends. Check quality of bombs and scores. Declare winner. (*5 minutes*)

5 *Review*
Points which should emerge will include:
a *Planning*
  • Did participants fully understand the scoring system and work out the optimum method of gaining points?
  • How did they calculate the number of bombs they could construct?
  • Did they attempt any practice construction? If so, how?
b *Application*
  • What were the participants' reactions if their calculations were inaccurate?
  • Could they see how their miscalculation arose?
  • How did this exercise relate to planning career structures and applying for jobs?
  (*15 minutes*)

1 The task

You are about to take part in a competition against the other participants. The competition contains two elements:

a to make as many water bombs as you can in 20 minutes according to the design you have been given;

b to calculate and declare how many bombs you will be able to make in that time.

2 Scoring

a for every water bomb you make you score 50 points

b for every water bomb you make *in excess* of the number you declared, 10 points are deducted

c for every bomb you make *less than* the number you declared, 20 points are deducted

d the participant with the highest score at the end of 20 minutes is the winner

3 Planning

You have 10 minutes in which to plan your course of action. At the end of 10 minutes you are to complete the attached tear-off slip and hand it to your tutor, from whom you will also collect paper for the construction of the bombs. When all the slips have been collected, the tutor will give the signal for the competition to begin.

NAME _____

NUMBER OF BOMBS
TO BE COMPLETED
IN 20 MINUTES _____

WATER BOMB 1
Construction sheet

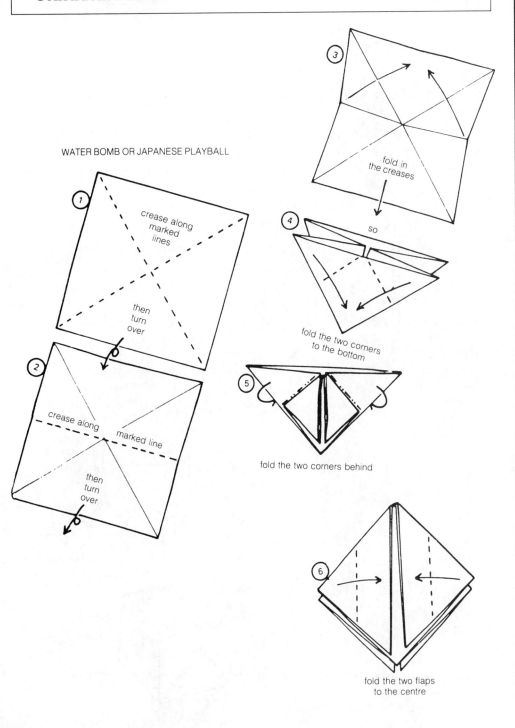

WATER BOMB OR JAPANESE PLAYBALL

1 crease along marked lines

then turn over

2 crease along marked line

then turn over

3 fold in the creases

4 so

fold the two corners to the bottom

5 fold the two corners behind

6 fold the two flaps to the centre

WATER BOMB 1
Construction sheet   *continued*

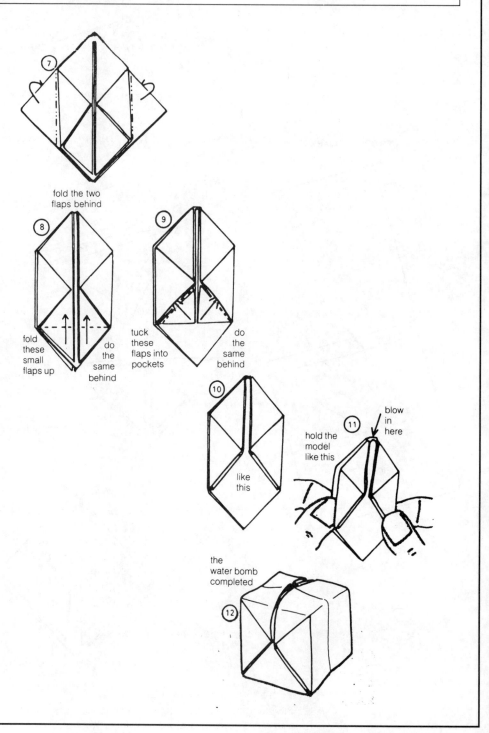

fold the two
flaps behind

fold
these
small
flaps up

do
the
same
behind

tuck
these
flaps into
pockets

do
the
same
behind

like
this

hold the
model
like this

blow
in
here

the
water bomb
completed

WATER BOMB 2

Objectives
- to examine behaviour and organisation within a group
- to help participants realise the importance of a realistic assessment of their skills, capabilities and experience

Description
Groups in competition are asked to calculate how many water bombs they can make in 20 minutes. They then make the bombs and compare the outcome with their forecasts.

Target group
Years 4–5, 6th form, staff

Organisation
Groups of 4. One/two tutors plus observers

Time required
1 hour. This can be extended with a longer *Review*.

Tutor skills
This exercise can be tackled by tutors with little previous experience.

Location
Any room large enough to give the individuals adequate working space.

Materials
One briefing sheet per group
One *Water Bomb* construction sheet per group
Paper for construction (A4 size tests manipulative skills; larger will test use of space)

Tutor's notes

1 Issue each group with a briefing sheet and two *Water Bomb* construction sheets. Remind them that they have 10 minutes for planning. Tell them the quality of construction you will expect. Give them any instructions you think necessary about timing (the dynamics can be noticeably different if you time them, if they time themselves, or if nothing is said about timing at all). (*15 minutes*)

2 Collect in declaration tear-off strips. Dispose of all trial bombs. Issue paper. Announce start of construction time. (*5 minutes*)

3 Groups work on task. (*20 minutes*)

4 Task ends. Check quality of bombs and scores. Declare winner. (*5 minutes*)

5 *Review*
Points which should emerge will include:
a *Planning*
  - Did groups fully understand the scoring system and work out the optimum method of gaining points?
  - How did they calculate the number of bombs they could construct?
  - Did they attempt any practice construction? If so, how?
b *Execution*
  - Did the groups stick to the plan they had made?
  - What happened if they found they were failing to meet their targets?
  - Any relevant inter-personal behaviour?
c *Application*
  - What were the participants' reactions if their calculations were inaccurate?
  - Could they see how their miscalculation arose?
  - Did participants see in this exercise any relationship to career planning and job application? (*15 minutes*)

WATER BOMB 2
Briefing sheet

1 The task
You are about to take part in a competition against the other groups. The competition contains two elements:

a to make as many water bombs as you can in 20 minutes according to the design you have been given;

b to calculate and declare how many bombs you will be able to make in that time.

2 Scoring
a for every water bomb you make you score 50 points

b for every water bomb you make *in excess* of the number you declared, 10 points are deducted

c for every bomb you make *less than* the number you declared, 20 points are deducted

d the group with the highest score at the end of 20 minutes is the winner

3 Planning
You have 10 minutes in which to plan your course of action. At the end of 10 minutes you are to complete the attached tear-off slip and hand it to your tutor, from whom you will also collect paper for the construction of the bombs. When all the slips have been collected, the tutor will give the signal for the competition to begin.

GROUP MEMBERS   _____

NUMBER OF BOMBS
TO BE COMPLETED
IN 20 MINUTES   _____

© Bill Dennison, Roger Kirk   Blackwell   1990

TRIPLE CROWN

Objectives
- to improve skills in planning, establishing priorities and setting targets
- to help evaluate individual and group skills
- to enable groups to discuss the requirements of successful team-building and teamwork

Description
Groups in competition are asked to undertake simultaneously three tasks requiring different skills. Before commencing the tasks they are required to state what they consider to be the potential of their group, either in terms of productivity or of speed of working.

Target group
Staff – possibly 6th form

Organisation
Groups of 6–8. One/two tutors plus one observer per group

Time required
1½ hours

Tutor skills
This exercise should only be tackled by tutors with considerable experience.

Location
Any room large enough to give the individuals adequate working space.

Materials
For each group:
Two briefing sheets
Two *Water Bomb* construction sheets
Paper (A4 or larger)
One jigsaw (100–150 pieces)
One/two *The Siding* briefing sheets

Tutor's notes

1 Divide the participants into groups of 6–8 and allocate them to working areas within the room. Issue each group with two briefing sheets and the other materials outlined above. (*5 minutes*)

2 Groups work on their plans. Check that they haven't started to construct water bombs or to solve *The Siding* and that they haven't opened the jigsaw box. (*25 minutes*)

3 Collect target sheets. Announce the start of working time. Ask observers to time their groups and to note completion of jigsaw and *The Siding*. (*25 minutes*)

4 Competition ends. Check scores. Declare winner. (*5 minutes*)

5 *Review*
Ask groups to consider the following:
a Planning
- How did the group structure itself and allocate tasks?
- Was any check made as to the relevant skills and experience of individual members of the group?
- Was the scoring system fully understood?
- Was an attempt made to evaluate the respective scoring potential of each of the three tasks?
b The task
- Did the group keep to its plan? If not, why not?
- When any one of the tasks was completed, what did those involved in it then do? Why? Was there any relevant inter-personal behaviour?

c *Application*
  • How did the group react if its targets proved to be inaccurate?
  • Could it see how its miscalculation arose?
  • Could it suggest methods of improvement?
  (*30 minutes*)

TRIPLE CROWN
Briefing sheet

---

1 The task

You are about to take part in a competition against the other groups. The competition includes three elements:

a • to make as many water bombs as you can in 25 minutes according to the design you have been given;
   • to calculate and disclose how many bombs you will be able to make in that time;

b • to complete a small jigsaw puzzle;
   • to calculate and disclose how long this will take you;

c • to solve the problem *The Siding*;
   • to calculate and disclose how long this will take you.

2 Planning

You have 25 minutes in which to plan your course of action and to calculate your targets. Your tutors has given you a *Water Bomb* construction sheet, a jigsaw and *The Siding*. You may look at these to help your planning, but you may not start on any of the activities or open the jigsaw box until the tutor tells you that the competition has started.

At the end of 15 minutes you are to fill in your target sheet and hand it to the tutor. When all the target sheets have been collected a signal will be given for the competition to begin.

3 Scoring

a   Water bomb construction
     • for every water bomb you make you score 50 points;
     • for every bomb you make *in excess* of the number you declared, 10 points are deducted;
     • for every bomb you make *less than* the number you declared, 20 points are deducted.

b Jigsaw
     • for completing the jigsaw in:
     less than 25 minutes you score 250 points
     less than 20 minutes you score 300 points
     less than 15 minutes you score 375 points
     less than 10 minutes you score 500 points.

- for completion within one minute of your target time there is a bonus of 50 points;
- for every minute more or less than this you lose 10 points, whether you have completed the jigsaw or not.

c The Siding
- for solving the problem in:
  less than 25 minutes you score 250 points
  less than 20 minutes you score 300 points
  less than 15 minutes you score 375 points
  less than 10 minutes you score 500 points.
- for a solution within one minute of your target time there is a bonus of 50 points;
- for every minute more or less than this you lose 10 points whether you have solved the problem or not.

d At the end of 25 minutes the scores from all three activities will be added together and the group with the highest total will be the winner.

TRIPLE CROWN
Target sheet

Group _____

1 Water bombs:

We will construct _____ bombs in 25 minutes.

2 Jigsaw:

We will complete the jigsaw in _____ minutes.

3 The Siding:

We will solve the problem in _____ minutes.

THE SIDING

Objective • to consider behaviour and organisation within a group

Target group Older pupils in schools, FE students, staff and other adult groups

Tutor's notes

The solution to the problem is as follows:

Weight (tons)	8	10	7	12	9
Destination	Bradford	Exeter	Stratford	Holyhead	Arbroath
Contents	Shovels	Prams	Fish	Books	Drums
Day	Friday	Thursday	Tuesday	Monday	Wednesday
Colour	Blue	Green	Red	Yellow	White

Hence the books are going to **Holyhead** and the Bradford wagon weighs **8 tons**.

The logic of the solution is as follows. (If a full understanding of the logic is required, it may be helpful to have a blank of the above diagram available, and to build up the information as it is determined.)

Statement number	Deduction
15	First wagon – Monday. Wagons arrive on consecutive days; therefore last wagon arrived on Friday.
13	Wagon on extreme left must have arrived on Friday.
3	Extreme right must be Wednesday.
9	Centre wagon – Tuesday.
6	Exeter next to Friday, therefore Exeter second from left.
8	Exeter not first, therefore not Monday. Therefore second wagon from right – Monday, therefore Exeter wagon – Thursday.
2	Monday wagon must have yellow sticker.
12	Second to arrive – fish, therefore Tuesday – fish.
16	Prams next to fish, must be either Monday or Thursday, BUT:
14	Pram wagon has green sticker, therefore NOT Monday. Therefore prams – Thursday – green.
11	Bradford – shovels, BUT:
19	Shovels not on Wednesday. Therefore Bradford is either Friday or Monday, BUT:
1	Arbroath and Holyhead wagons are together, therefore Bradford cannot be Monday, therefore Bradford – Friday – shovels.
5	Drums – white sticker, can only be Wednesday.
10	Stratford – red sticker, must be Tuesday. Therefore Bradford must have blue sticker (elimination).

18	Exeter wagon must weigh 10 tons.
4	Books – 12 tons, must be Monday wagon (elimination).
7	Arbroath – 9 tons, therefore must be Wednesday. Therefore Monday must be Holyhead. First question answered.
17	7 ton truck to the right (not necessarily immediately) of the 8 ton truck. Therefore Bradford – 8 tons, Stratford – 7 tons. Second question answered and problem solved.

This exercise is useful in studying group dynamics in a confusing situation. There is a high element of difficulty in tackling a problem of this nature as a group, because individual trains of thought are very difficult to maintain. If each member of the group is given a copy of the problem, there may be a tendency for individual working, although the complexity usually produces cries for help. Alternatively, it may be useful to issue a limited number of copies, to ensure that at least small group working takes place. The benefit of the exercise is entirely in the process analysis which should follow. This may lead to considerable examination of relationships.

THE SIDING
Student's briefing sheet

A railway siding can be entered from either end. There are five trucks in the siding, all with different destinations and contents. They all have different gross weights and different-coloured trade advertisement stickers. The trucks arrived in the siding on different, but consecutive days. The following facts are known:

1 The trucks for Holyhead and Arbroath are together.

2 The truck with the yellow sticker arrived first.

3 The truck on the extreme right was the third to arrive.

4 The 12 ton truck contains books.

5 The truck containing drums has a white sticker.

6 The truck for Exeter is next to the truck which arrived on Friday.

7 The Arbroath truck weighs 9 tons.

8 The truck for Exeter did not arrive first.

9 The truck in the middle arrived on Tuesday.

10 The Stratford truck has a red sticker.

11 The shovels are going to Bradford.

12 The second wagon to arrive contains fish.

13 The last truck to arrive is on the extreme left.

14 The truck with the green sticker contains prams.

15 The first wagon arrived on Monday.

16 The prams are next to the fish.

17 The 7 ton truck is to the right of the 8 ton truck.

18 The truck with the blue sticker is beside the truck weighing 10 tons.

19 The shovels did not arrive on Wednesday.

Where are the books going?

How heavy is the Bradford wagon?

CAPITATION COMMITTEE

Objective	• to improve negotiating, influencing and consensus skills
Description	As the title implies, this problem explores the allocation of funds within a school. Participants represent individual departments and are required to negotiate a satisfactory solution.
Target group	Staff, possibly 6th form
Organisation	Groups of 5 One/two tutors plus observers
Time required	1¼ hours
Tutor skills	This exercise can be tackled by tutors with little previous experience.
Location	Any room in which groups can work with reasonable privacy.
Materials	One briefing sheet per participant. (Sheets are in sets of five, all different.)

Tutor's notes

1 Distribute briefing sheets. Allow groups five minutes to plan their courses of action. (*10 minutes*)

2 Groups work on problem (*35–45 minutes*)

3 *Review*
   Points which should emerge will include:
   • How did the group organise itself?
   • How was the money distributed?
   • What factors influenced the group's decision?
   • Who influenced whom? How?
   • How did individuals cope when they were asked for information that was not in the briefing sheets?
   • Any relevant inter-personal behaviour?
   (*30 minutes*)

CAPITATION COMMITTEE
Briefing sheet

You are a member of the Capitation Committee of Swann Upper School. Under Local Management of Schools an additional sum of £3,500 has been set aside to provide extra resources to assist departments which are involved in new curricular initiatives, such as the introduction of new courses, or which have particular needs. You have met to allocate this money.

You represent the Language Department whose normal capitation is £2,274. You are committed to the introduction of foreign languages to a wider cross-section of the school in accordance with the National Curriculum, and are anxious to engage in GCSE examinations in both French and German. This will involve new courses and textbooks in the 4th year which certainly cannot be provided from normal capitation. Two sets of *Reisepass* will cost £370. *Tricolore 4* is more expensive (£814.45) as it includes two pupils' books and also films, tapes and teacher's book.

With these new courses you anticipate a growth of interest in Languages among pupils and a consequent improvement in examination results.

CAPITATION COMMITTEE
Briefing sheet

You are a member of the Capitation Committee of Swann Upper School. Under Local Management of Schools an additional sum of £3,500 has been set aside to provide extra resources to assist departments which are involved in new curricular initiatives, such as the introduction of new courses, or which have particular needs. You have met to allocate this money.

You represent the Science Department, which has been placed in extreme financial difficulty by the introduction of Balanced Science. This has resulted in an increased uptake for GCSE courses which are expensive to resource. For instance, next year's 5th form has to be provided with electronic equipment costing £920.

In addition, the Department has lost a temporary laboratory/classroom which had been used for Rural Science units for the NPRA curriculum for pupils of less ability. This resource needs replacing with a greenhouse equipped with power and water at a cost in the region of £400. These sums simply cannot be found out of your capitation of £3,661.

© Bill Dennison, Roger Kirk   Blackwell   1990

You are a member of the Capitation Committee of Swann Upper School. Under Local Management of Schools an additional sum of £3,500 has been set aside to provide extra resources to assist departments which are involved in new curricular initiatives, such as the introduction of new courses, or which have particular needs. You have met to allocate this money.

You represent the Business Studies Department. As you only teach pupils in the 4th, 5th and 6th forms, your capitation is a mere £962. You are about to set up a new GCSE Business and Information Studies course in the 4th form and to expand the Secretarial 6th. Both the GCSE and 6th form courses require 'hands-on' computer experience, and you will be catering for a maximum of 20 pupils at any one time. As the Department at present only has 5 machines (a ration of 1 to 4 for the 4th form and 1 to 2 for the 6th) and each 6th former needs 4 hours a week on a machine, resources are clearly inadequate. Another 5 computer units are needed at a cost of £815 per unit.

© Bill Dennison, Roger Kirk   Blackwell   1990

CAPITATION COMMITTEE
Briefing sheet

You are a member of the Capitation Committee of Swann Upper School. Under Local Management of Schools an additional sum of £3,500 has been set aside to provide extra resources to assist departments which are involved in new curricular initiatives, such as the introduction of new courses, or which have particular needs. You have met to allocate this money.

You represent the Craft, Design and Technology Department, which urgently needs to convert an existing traditional workshop into a second Technology Room. The conversion of the first room, funded by the Authority, has been highly successful in raising pupils' interest and awareness of technology, but this very success has created problems. Priority has to be given to pupils taking the GCSE *CDT: Technology* course in the 4th and 5th forms, which means that many pupils in the 1st, 2nd and 3rd forms do not get a chance to use the room at all. Enthusiasm for this vital subject is being stifled as pupils have to undertake electronic projects in an unsuitable basic workshop, which they feel to be quite the wrong context.

Conversion of this room into a multi-media workshop with facilities both for technology and for work of a more traditional nature would involve the following expenditure:

Iroko side benching	£380.00
Under bench storage units	£505.00
Additional power sockets (say)	£100.00
Bubble Etch Tank	£159.00
UV (Ultra-violet) exposure unit	£67.50
General equipment (soldering irons etc)	£230.00

You gather that the Authority is not prepared to provide any further special funding, but a private charitable trust has offered £500, on condition that the school produces the remainder of the money. The Department's normal capitation is £1,768.

CAPITATION COMMITTEE
Briefing sheet

You are a member of the Capitation Committee of Swann Upper School. Under Local Management of Schools an additional sum of £3,500 has been set aside to provide extra resources to assist Departments which are involved in new curricular initiatives, such as the introduction of new courses, or which have particular needs. You have met to allocate this money.

You represent the English Department which this year has a special problem brought about by the introduction of new examination set texts. At 'A' level, for instance, where you expect about 15 students, you have to buy copies of Chaucer and Coleridge, *King Lear* and *Othello*, *The Return of the Native* and *Catch 22*. Even by using paperbacks where available, the total cost will be £785.45. GCSE texts, where changes are less, will cost a further £205.50.

The total capitation of the Department is only £3,095, which is comfortably taken up by texts for general study throughout the school, course books and stationery.

The English Department consistently has some of the best examination results in the school, yet during a recent visit of HMI adverse comment was expressed about the age and condition of many of the books in regular use.

DARLINGTON STATION

Objective   • to provide a vehicle for study of group processes in a task activity

Target group   Older pupils in schools, FE students, teachers and other adult groups

Materials   One briefing sheet for each member of the group. (Sheets are in sets of six, all slightly different. For the tutor's benefit they can be distinguished by the number of full stops at the end of the first paragraph.)
One *Operating Track Network* diagram per group.

Tutor's notes

The exercise is not primarily designed to display problem-solving techniques, because the primary task is defined, and the solution specified. The problem faced by a group is fundamentally that of data handling, and group effectiveness will depend upon inter-personal dynamics, such as role allocation. To this extent therefore the final completion of the task (or the accuracy of the solution) is secondary, though likely to be of considerable importance to the participants.

Process

1 Groups of six should be used wherever possible.

2 Group formation may be:
   • by direction
   • by participant choice (introducing further elements of behaviour)
   • by some other process, designed to elicit some behavioural dynamic.

3 Issue each group with one of the six briefing sheets and one copy of the *Operating Track Network*. Groups should be able to work without interference/distraction.

4 Process observers should watch each syndicate. It may be possible for participants to fill this role, especially if the total members are not divisible by six, but observers thus identified should be carefully briefed beforehand. Alternatively, 'extra' participants may be included in syndicates, and given a duplicate briefing sheet.

5 Timing of the exercise cannot be predicted precisely. A complex problem is involved, and the satisfactory solution, although desirable, is not essential. Time set aside for *Review* of the behavioural learning should therefore be preserved.

6 Process observation should include some indentification of:
   a) The roles adopted by members: chairman, time-keeper, comedian, technician, specialist etc. How were these roles identified within the group? Were they simply assumed by individuals? What control did the group exercise? To what effect? Were there any conflicts or restricted bids for power/control? What effect did these have on the group (motivationally or in terms of effectiveness)?
   b) The development of the group. Can a group's 'life' be traced? Through what stages (confusion, despair, optimism, excitement)? What incidents changed the group ethos, and were these changes attributable to specific actions by individual members? The manner in which the group was formed will clearly influence the early stages, when a stranger group will be partially concerned with problems associated with discomfort, reticence, premature bids for leadership and so on.

7 The discovery that different members have different information is an important turning point, and particular note should be taken of when and how the discovery was made. The work pattern of the group is likely to change dramatically at this point and new roles may emerge. Data is therefore likely to be abundant, and should be carefully observed and recorded.

8 Tutors will, of course, play back their data to the group during the *Review* stage in accordance with their own style. A useful strategy is to ask the group to recall their own data on some of the issues identified in 6 above, and consider the learning which can be associated with such incidents. The tutor's notes of the process – which should include quotations and times – can help to clarify any confusion, but should not, of course, be used to arbitrate in any dispute, nor in a facetious or damaging way.

9 The design element which gives different syndicate members different data is intended to mirror real-life situations. Although in working, group members may believe that they share common data, communication and/or value system problems often produce wide variations in contribution. It is intended that many groups will find this feature educational.

The problem

The main problem is that all traffic movements through the station are hampered by a bottleneck (point A on the *Operating Track Network* sheet). To handle the necessary data, a graphical representation of traffic movements (including those past point A) is almost essential (see the *Time Limits* diagram on page 169). (Graph paper should be available to syndicates on request.) This representation shows the times available for the special train movements.

The solution detailed below may not be the only one, but it does comply with all the requirements. Alternatives generated may be closely checked, depending upon whether the correct solution is a major dynamic of the exercise.

The separate processes involved are:

1 Locomotive moving from shed to carriages.
   Two options exist.
   a) Direct, avoiding platform 4
      Time taken =

Signals/points	1 minute
Movement to carriages	2 minutes
Couple up	2 minutes
Total	5 minutes

If this movement commences at 09 00, it is therefore completed by 09 05.
   b) Via platform 4.
      Since a parcels train is due to arrive in platform 4 at 09 00, the locomotive cannot move through the platform between 09 00 and

09 05. However, after the parcels train departs (at 09 20) the locomotive can leave the shed, and proceed to the carriages, and will be coupled up by 09 25.

Commence	09 20
Signals/points	1 minute
Travel to carriage	2 minutes
Couple up	2 minutes

Completed by 09 25

2 Special train moves out of platform 4.

Irrespective of whether a) or b) above is used, this movement cannot commence until the parcels train has left platform 4.

Timing thereafter is:

		Option a)	Option b)
Movement commences		09 20	09 25
Signals/points	1 minute	09 21	09 26
Move to platform 4	2 minutes	09 23	09 28
Uncouple	2 minutes	09 25	09 30
Signals/points	1 minute	09 26	09 31
Loco travels to shed	2 minutes	09 28	09 33
Signals/points	1 minute	09 29	09 34
Loco travels to S of carriage siding	2 minutes	09 31	09 36
Signals/points	1 minute	09 32	09 37
Loco travels to S of platform 4	2 minutes	09 34	09 39
Couples up	2 minutes	09 36	09 41
Signals/points	1 minute	09 37	09 42
Train travels to head shunt	2 minutes	09 39	09 44

Since the Newcastle train is due to arrive in platform 4 at 09 45, option b) is now seen to be unuseable – because the necessary 5 minutes clearance does not exist.

The movements incorporated above are necessary for the following reasons:

- The special must use platform 4 to escape from the carriage siding.
- The locomotive will, however, be at the northern end of the train, and since it must precede (ie pull, not push) the train to Leeds (southwards) it is necessary for the locomotive to 'run round' the carriages. This is only possible on platform 4.
- Platform 4 must be vacated by 09 40, to allow the Newcastle train to enter. Escape from platform 4 northwards is not an option, because the special could not (subsequently) travel south on the main (through lines). It is not possible for the train to leave from platform 4 direct to Leeds at 09 40 because of the passage of the (southbound) express at 09 40. The only alternative therefore is to use the head shunt.

3 Special train moves to departure platform.
Due to movement of other trains past point A, the special cannot leave
the head shunt until 10 10. It has the option of going to either platforms
1 or 4 at that time, although logic suggests that since platform 1 is used
for southbound trains, it should also be used by the special.
Timing of this movement is:

Signals/points	1 minute	10 11
Moves to platform 1	2 minutes	10 13
Waits 6 minutes (fulfills		
boarding requirements)		10 19
Signals/points	1 minute	10 20
Departs		10 20

The answers to the (various) questions asked of the syndicate are:
a) The special should use platform 1 (platform 4 also possible).
b) The special should leave Darlington at 10 20.★
c) The special should be positioned for boarding at 10 13.

★ Points set after boarding time because of other (ie shunting) movements.
Thus points set only when the train is in – (theoretically) loaded. The
loading time (for work study purposes) is separate from the setting time
(in practice the train is at the platform for seven minutes).

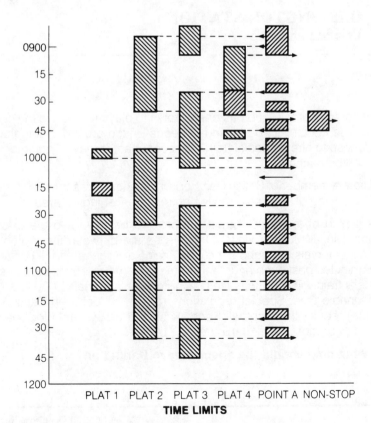

PLAT 1   PLAT 2   PLAT 3   PLAT 4   POINT A   NON-STOP
TIME LIMITS

DARLINGTON STATION
Briefing sheet

Darlington Football Club has been drawn to play Liverpool in the semi-final of the FA Cup. The match is to be played at Leeds United ground. Darlington FC Supporters' Club wish to hire a special train of six coaches, to leave Darlington for Leeds on the day of the match.

You are a member of British Rail's operations team, responsible for the co-ordination and planning of rail traffic movements in the Darlington area.

The timing of the special train will have to be fitted into the existing schedule of trains. Diesel Multiple Units (DMUs) operate between Darlington and Saltburn at regular intervals throughout the day. Trains are scheduled to arrive at platform 3 at 25 minutes past each hour, and at platform 2 at 55 minutes past each hour. Both these platforms are designed for DMU operation, and are only long enough to accept a five coach train (plus locomotive).

Which platform should be used for the football special?

DARLINGTON STATION
Briefing sheet

Darlington Football Club has been drawn to play Liverpool in the semi-final of the FA Cup. The match is to be played at Leeds United ground. Darlington FC Supporters' Club wish to hire a special train of six coaches, to leave Darlington for Leeds on the day of the match . .

You are a member of British Rail's operations team, responsible for the co-ordination and planning of rail traffic movements in the Darlington area.

The timing of the special train will have to be fitted into the existing schedule of trains. Diesel Multiple Units (DMUs) operate between Darlington and Saltburn at regular intervals throughout the day. Trains are scheduled to depart from platform 3 at 5 minutes past each hour, and from platform 2 at 35 minutes past each hour. The special train will need to leave Darlington not later than 11.30 to arrive in Leeds at a reasonable time. Special regulations (drawn up between British Rail and the civil Police) require that Football Specials should be available for boarding for not less than 5, nor more than 10 minutes.

At what time should the special leave Darlington?

DARLINGTON STATION
Briefing sheet

Darlington Football Club has been drawn to play Liverpool in the semi-final of the FA Cup. The match is to be played at Leeds United ground. Darlington FC Supporters' Club wish to hire a special train of six coaches to leave Darlington for Leeds on the day of the match . . .

You are a member of British Rail's operations team, responsible for the co-ordination and planning of rail traffic movements in the Darlington area.

The special train will have to be timed to fit into the existing scheduled services. Three trains will be using platform 4 on the day in question; the Newcastle parcels train, due to arrive at 09.00 and depart at 09.20; an Inter-City express arriving at 09.45 and departing for Newcastle at 09.50, and a further express for Durham, Newcastle and Edinburgh, due to arrive at 10.45 and depart at 10.50.

The coaches for the special train will be prepared by the Carriage group, cleaned, inspected and parked in the carriage siding, on the day before the match.

At what time should the special train be positioned on a platform so that the soccer fans can board?

Darlington Football Club has been drawn to play Liverpool in the semi-final of the FA Cup. The match is to be played at Leeds United ground. Darlington FC Supporters' Club wish to hire a special train of six coaches to leave Darlington for Leeds on the day of the match . . . .

You are a member of British Rail's operations team, responsible for the co-ordination and planning of rail traffic movements in the Darlington area.

The special train will have to be timed to fit into the existing schedule of regular services. Trains travelling South through Darlington on the morning of the match are: the Inter-City express for York and Kings Cross, due to arrive at platform 1 at 09.55, and depart at 10.00; a slow parcels train, due to arrive at platform 1 at 10.30, and depart at 10.40, and the Kings Cross express, due to arrive at platform 1 at 11.00 and depart at 11.00.

You should remember that any train travelling on the main line must be pulled by a locomotive (ie it can't be pushed from the rear) because visibility from modern diesel locomotives is very restricted. However, on the day in question, no spare 'shunting' locomotive is available. So the locomotive allocated for the special train will have to marshall the coaches inside the station network, and during such movements, it is permissible for the coaches to be 'pushed' for short distances. The loco for the special will be available in the loco shed at 09.00, the time when its crew are due to report for duty.

At what time should the special leave Darlington?

© Bill Dennison, Roger Kirk   Blackwell   1990

DARLINGTON STATION
Briefing sheet

Darlington Football Club has been drawn to play Liverpool in the semi-final of the FA Cup. The match is to be played at Leeds United ground. Darlington FC Supporters' Club wish to hire a special train of six coaches to leave Darlington for Leeds on the day of the match . . . . .

You are a member of British Rail's operations team, responsible for the co-ordination and planning of rail traffic movements in the Darlington area.

The movements of the football special will have to be arranged to harmonise with scheduled trains. On the morning of the match, there is one non-stop train, from Newcastle to Kings Cross, which is due to pass Darlington (on the through tracks east of the station) at 09.40. Its speed at this point will be approximately 95 mph.

You know that when local traffic movements are being planned, work study timings must be used. Once a locomotive has signalled its readiness to move, it takes one minute for the necessary signals and points to be set. A single non-stop movement between any two points within the station can then be made in 2 minutes, and it takes 2 minutes to couple (or uncouple) a locomotive to passenger coaches. Thus if a locomotive wants to move from the shed to platform 3, 1 minute should be allowed for points, 2 minutes to travel to beyond the platform 3 points, 1 minute again for points setting, and 2 minutes for the movement. Thus 6 minutes would be required in total.

How long will it take to prepare the special train? At what time will it depart?

Darlington Football Club has been drawn to play Liverpool in the semi-final of the FA Cup. The match is to be played at Leeds United ground. Darlington FC Supporters' Club wish to hire a special train of six coaches to leave Darlington for Leeds on the day of the match . . . . . .

You are a member of British Rail's operations team, responsible for the co-ordination and planning of all rail traffic movements in the Darlington area.

The movement of the football special will have to be fitted into the pattern of existing scheduled services using the station on the day in question. Very strict regulations exist governing the safety margins of train movements. Within the station network, if any piece of track is to be used by a scheduled service then no other rail traffic is allowed to use any part of that track in the five minutes preceding the scheduled movement. Furthermore, since all route points and signals must be correctly positioned, the whole route is regarded as being in use at the scheduled movement time. Thus if a train is due to arrive at (say) platform 1 from Saltburn at 12.00, the track from Saltburn to platform 1 is regarded as occupied at 12.00, and no other movement can be made on any part of it after 11.55. In other words the time taken by the incoming train to travel the required distance is irrelevant. As far as the main lines to the east of the station are concerned, the safety margins are even more stringent. The track must be empty for five minutes before the passage of a non-stop express, and for five minutes afterwards – to allow for the train being early or late.

No scheduled service can be delayed or re-timed in order to accommodate the football special.

At what time should the special leave Darlington?

DARLINGTON STATION
Operating track network

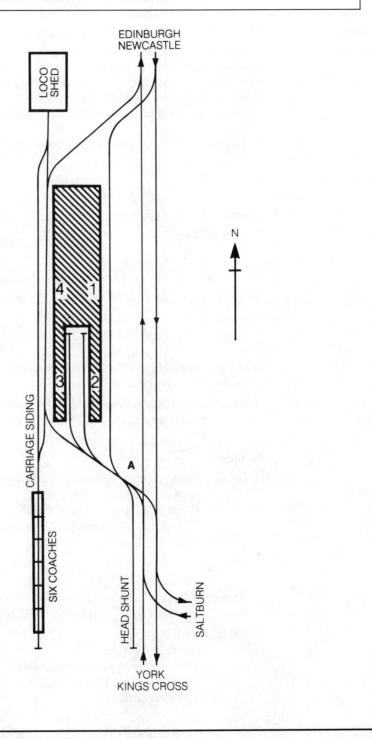

LOCO SHED

EDINBURGH
NEWCASTLE

N

4 1

3 2

A

CARRIAGE SIDING

SIX COACHES

HEAD SHUNT

SALTBURN

YORK
KINGS CROSS

THE INDIVISIBLE LOAD

Objectives
- to provide an opportunity to consider communication, leadership, and other group processes.

Target group   Older pupils in schools, FE students, teachers and other adult groups.

Organisation   Groups of six should be used wherever possible. The group may nominate a leader who should be given the map only. The other five group members should each be issued with a separate briefing sheet. (The briefing sheets are all slightly different. For the tutor's benefit they can be distinguished by the number of full stops at the end of the first paragraph.)
For groups with more than six members, duplicate briefing sheets should be issued.

Time   At least 1½ hours.

Tutor's notes: solution
Essential Data

	Height	Total height	Axles	Axle weight	Speed
Bogey Type A	0.71m	5.77m	4	9.25 tonnes	2 mph
B	1.07m	6.12m	4	9.25 tonnes	5 mph
C	1.29m	6.35m	6	6.17 tonnes	2 mph

Total time available 07.45 – 04.35 = 190 minutes. (07.45 is latest arrival time; 04.35 is end of darkness.)

Bridge under railway is limited to 5.94m – only type A used.
Bridge over railway is limited to 3 tonnes/axle – cannot be used.

Solutions

1 Using Type A, crossing railway under bridge:

Shortest distance = 4½ miles	
Time @ 2 mph = 2 hours 15 minutes	= 135 mins
Delays: 5 × 90° turns @ 10 mins each	= 50 mins
Negotiate bridge	= 20 mins
Total time	= 205 mins
	= 3 hours 25 mins

To reach gates by 07.45, departure by 07.45–03.25 = 0420
Not daylight until 04.35 – NOT POSSIBLE.

2 Via level crossing

Shortest distance	= 5 miles
Delays: straight on at roundabout	= 30 mins
5 × 90° turns at 10 mins each	= 50 mins
Level crossing itself	= 20 mins
Total	= 100 mins
Fastest bogey (Type B) 5 mph time taken	= 60 mins

Total delays	= 100 mins
Total journey	= 160 mins
But L/C only available at certain times:	= 30 mins
Distance from works to L/C = 2½ miles	= 30 mins
Delays: 3 × 90° turns @ 10 mins	= 30 mins
Straight on at roundabout	= 90 mins
Time from works to L/C	= 1 hour 30 mins

L/C available at 05.40.
Must leave works at 05.40–01.30 = 0410 (TOO EARLY)
L/C available at 06.35.
Must leave works at 06.35–01.30 = 05.05
Then leave L/C (After 20 minute delay) = 06.55

Distance still to travel = 2½ miles	= 30 mins
Delays: 2 × 90° turns @ 10 mins	= 20 mins
	= 50 mins
Arrive at dock gates 06.55 + 50 mins	= 0745.

Insurance cost will be 160 mins × £10	= £1,600
Premium for using L/C	= £1,000
Total	= £2,600

Answers

Total insurance cost	£2,600
Time leaving works	0505
Route via L/C	
Arrival at dock gates	0745
Bogey used	Type B.

THE INDIVISIBLE LOAD
Briefing sheet

One of the problems facing an engineering firm is the transportation of a large steel vessel from the firm's works to the nearby Docks.

The vessel has the following dimensions:

Length: 26.5m   Diameter: 5.06m   Weight (including 2 bogies): 74 tonnes.

The vessel must be delivered to the Dock Gates no later than 07.45 hours. The major obstacle is the railway line: the bridge under this railway has headroom of 5.94m and the level crossing is very narrow.

Of the bogies available, Type A has the following specifications:

No. of axles   4
Height   0.71m
Max speed   2 mph.

The attached map shows the roads which might be used.

What time should the load leave the works?

THE INDIVISIBLE LOAD
Briefing sheet

One of the problems facing an engineering firm is the transportation of a large steel vessel from the firm's works to the nearby Docks. .

The vessel is an absorption column, which must be delivered to the Dock Gates no later than 07.45 hours. The major obstacle is a busy four-track railway. The bridge under the railway is very narrow, and 20 minutes should be allowed for the load to negotiate this bridge.

Of the bogies available, Type B has the following specifications:

No. of axles   4
Height   1.07m
Max speed   5 mph.

There is no bogey available capable of negotiating a corner of less than 90°. An insurance premium of £10 for every minute that this load is in transit will have to be paid.

The attached map shows the roads which might be used.

What time will the load actually arrive at the Dock Gates?

THE INDIVISIBLE LOAD
Briefing sheet

One of the problems facing an engineering firm is the transportation of a large steel vessel from the firm's works to the nearby Docks. . .

You know that with a load of this kind, many delays occur through having to manoeuvre around obstacles. For example it will take 30 minutes to go 'straight-on' at a roundabout, and 10 minutes to negotiate a 90° corner. It would take 20 minutes to negotiate the level crossing, because of the limited clearances.

Lighting-up time on the day in question is from 21.30 to 04.35.

The attached map shows the roads which might be used.

What will the total cost of insurance be?

THE INDIVISIBLE LOAD
Briefing sheet

One of the problems facing an engineering firm is the transportation of a large steel vessel from the firm's works to the nearby Docks. . . .

The major obstacle is a railway line. If you use the level crossing there is an additional insurance premium of £1,000 to pay. On the day in question, the crossing gates can only be kept open between the following times:

> 05.40 to 06.00
> 06.35 to 06.55
> 07.10 to 07.30.

The attached map shows the roads which might be used.

Which route should be taken?

THE INDIVISIBLE LOAD
Briefing sheet

One of the problems facing an engineering firm is the transportation of a large steel vessel from the firm's works to the nearby Docks. . . . .

The main obstacle is a busy main-line railway. The bridge over this railway is prohibited to vehicles with axle-loadings greater than 3 tonnes, and the level crossing has an effective width of only 5.20m.

Of the bogies available, Type C has the following specifications:

No. of axles   6
Height   1.30m
Max speed   2 mph.

By law, a load of this kind cannot be moved during the hours of darkness.

The attached map shows the roads which might be used.

Which bogey should be employed?

THE INDIVISIBLE LOAD
Map

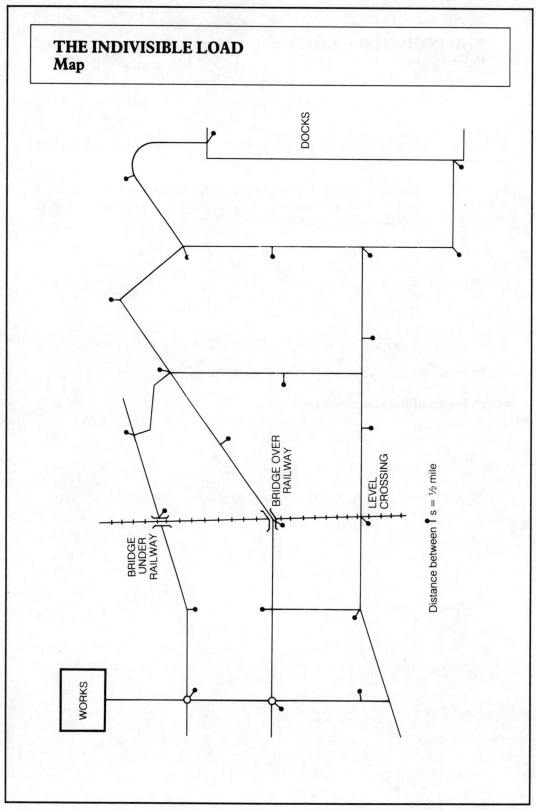

DOCKS

BRIDGE OVER RAILWAY

LEVEL CROSSING

BRIDGE UNDER RAILWAY

WORKS

Distance between •'s = ½ mile

PUSH–PULL

1 The objective of the exercise is for your group to finish up with a positive score.

or

The objective of the exercise is to beat the other group.

or

The objective of the exercise is to make (or lose) money for your group.

2 Imagine that there is a heavy weight in square B.2 of the grid. The combined efforts of the two teams will move the weight progressively into any of the squares in the grid. Each square shows the scores which will be awarded to each team if the weight is moved into that particular square.

	1		2		3		
RED	−3	RED	+3	RED	−6	**A**
BLUE	+6	BLUE	−3	RED	+3	
RED	+6	RED	+3	RED	−3	**B**
BLUE	−3	BLUE	+3	BLUE	+6	
RED	+6	RED	−3	RED	+6	**C**
BLUE	−6	BLUE	+6	BLUE	−3	

3 There are 12 rounds in the exercise. In each round, each team must make some effort to move the weight.

Each team may choose to push the weight either UP, DOWN, LEFT or RIGHT.

- If the groups push in opposite directions, the weight will not move.
- If the groups push in the same direction, the weight will move two squares or as far as possible within the confines of the grid.
- If the chosen directions are mutually at right angles, the weight will move one square diagonally.
- If any group attempts to push in a direction which would take the weight outside the confines of the grid, any such attempt will be regarded as though that group has not pushed at all, and the weight will move one square in the direction exerted by the other group.

4 No communications are permitted between the groups, except that after completing the fifth and tenth rounds, a representative from each group may meet for the purpose of negotiation. Ten minutes are allowed for round one, five minutes for round two, thereafter three minutes per round. All the time limits must be adhered to rigidly.

The fifth, tenth and twelfth rounds are bonus rounds. The scores awarded in round five will be twice the quoted scores; in round ten they are multiplied by three, and in round twelve they will be multiplied by five.

PUSH–PULL
Continued

5 If the financial element is added then the results of the exercises will be determined as follows:
  a Any group finishing with a minus score forfeits its stake to the tutor, who can donate the money to charity.
  b The group with the highest positive score keeps its own stake and is given the stake of the other group which finished with a lower positive score.
  c An additional bonus will be awarded by the tutor to any group which finishes with a score of +50 or more.
  d If both groups finish with identical scores, they both forfeit their stakes to the tutor (irrespective of the size of their scores) who can donate the money to charity. No bonus will be paid in this case.

PUSH–PULL
Score card

Weight starts in square B.2

Round No	Red effort	Blue effort	Weight to square No.	Red score	Blue score	Red total	Blue total
1							
2							
3							
4							
5*							
6							
7							
8							
9							
10*							
11							
12*							

* Denotes bonus round.

SUM

1 The objective of the exercise is for your team to score positively.

or

The objective of the exercise is for your team to beat the other two teams.

or

The objective of the exercise is to make (or lose) money for your team.

2 Each team for this exercise 'OWNS' two numbers:

RED team owns the numbers 1 and 6
BLUE team owns the numbers 2 and 5
GREEN team owns the numbers 3 and 4.

3 In each of the ten rounds of the exercise, each team must choose to use only *one* of its numbers. The choice must be made without the knowledge of the other two teams. The combined sum of the numbers used by all three teams in each round will determine the points awarded to each team as follows:

SUM of numbers played	Red score	Blue score	Green score
6	+3	+3	+3
7	−3	+3	+6
9	+3	+6	−3
10	+3	−3	+6
11	+6	−3	+3
12	+6	+3	−3
14	−3	+6	+3
15	−3	−3	−3

4 The fourth, seventh and tenth rounds carry bonus scores. In the fourth round, the points awarded will be double those shown; in the seventh round they will be multiplied by three, and in the tenth round by five.

5 No communication is permitted between the teams, except that after completion of the fourth and seventh rounds, a period of ten minutes will be made available for meetings to take place between one representative from each team for the purpose of negotiation.

© Bill Dennison, Roger Kirk   Blackwell   1990

SUM
Continued

6 Ten minutes will be allowed for round one, five minutes each for rounds two, three, four and five, thereafter three minutes per round. These times must be rigidly enforced.

7 Use the score sheet provided to record the progress of the exercise.

8 If the financial element is added the result of the exercise will be decided as follows:
   a The team with the highest positive score takes the stakes of all other team(s) with positive scores.
   b If two teams share the highest positive score, they each keep their own stakes, and share the stake of any team with a lower positive score.
   c If all three teams finish with identical positive scores, they all forfeit their stakes to the tutor, who can donate the sum to charity.
   d Any team finishing with a negative score forfeits its stake to the tutor, who can donate the money to charity.
   e If the arithmetic total of the three final scores is +120 or more, the tutors will award a bonus to the team(s) with the highest positive score.

SUM
Score sheet

Round number	Red choice	Blue choice	Green choice	Total (Sum)	Red score	Blue score	Green score	Red total	Blue total	Green total
1										
2										
3										
4*										
5										
6										
7*										
8										
9										
10*										

* Denotes bonus round.

Tutor's notes
The following table has been found to be of considerable assistance to
tutors running this exercise. It enables the results of each round to be
determined very quickly, and reduces the possibility of errors being made.
Since it demonstrates all the possible combinations, it is worthy of detailed
consideration from the point of view of examining the options and
strategies open to any group in any situation. To familiarise themselves
with these options, it is recommended that tutors 'play' the exercise
themselves, trying to identify with each of the competing syndicates in
turn.

Red choice	Blue choice	Green choice	Sum	Red score	Blue score	Green score
1	2	3	6	+3	+3	+3
1	2	4	7	−3	+3	+6
1	5	3	9	+3	+6	−3
1	5	4	10	+3	−3	+3
6	2	3	11	+6	−3	+3
6	2	4	12	+6	+3	−3
6	5	3	14	−3	+6	+3
6	5	4	15	−3	−3	−3

Table 1

If any team plays its lowest number, they may score either +3, +3, +3 or
−3.
If any team plays its highest number, they may score either +6, +6, −3 or
−3.
The low number ('safe') is also likely to produce 1:2:3, where all three
score +3.
The high number ('win') is also likely to produce 6:5:4, where all three
score −3.

From the 'co-operative' situation, with 1:2:3, any team which changes its
choice will (providing the others do not change) immediately benefit to the
tune of +6. Hence the possibility of a double-cross exists.

From the ultimate 'competitive' situation of 6:5:4, if only one team
changes, they will suffer thereby – there must be a mutual decision to
change on the part of all three, which would then produce 1:2:3.

All other combinations have the following in common. No team alone can ensure that they will score +6. In each case, this is controlled by one other team. For example:

For *Red* to score +6, they must play 6, but *Blue* must play 2.
For *Blue* to score +6 they must play 5, but *Green* must play 3.
For *Green* to score +6 they must play 4, but *Red* must play 1.

Thus if two syndicates combine forces, they can totally prevent the third syndicate from gaining 6.

The option open to this third syndicate is to force one of the teams who have combined to suffer −3 in each round. This is best illustrated by the following:

Supposing *Red* and *Blue* have combined to defeat *Green*. *Red* continuously play 6. *Blue* play 2. With this situation, *Red* will always score +6. BUT if *Green* play 4, they suffer −3 in each round (6:2:4 = 12). If, however, *Green* change we get 6:2:3 and *Blue* are penalised −3. This exerts a pressure on the partnership between *Red* and *Blue*, which is increased if *Blue* notice that from 6:2:3 they could change to 6:5:3 and immediately gain +6.

Bonus system
The bonus system ensures that the bonus can only be won if there is a satisfactory agreement to play 1:2:3 for a substantial part of the exercise. This is achieved as follows:

Since we are concerned with the net score at the completion of the exercise it follows that three dissimilar modes of operation can be identified.

a) If the (unlikely) event arose where 6:5:4 was played in every round, the net score in each round would be −3, −3, −3 = −9. If the bonus rounds are included, the net score at the end of the exercise would be −153.
b) If the sum in every round were 6 (1:2:3) then in each round the net score would be +3, +3, +3 = +9. Including bonus rounds, this gives a maximum possible net score of +153.
c) In each round where a win/lose situation arises, the net score is +6, +3, −3 = +6. Maximum obtainable score is therefore +102.

This demonstrates that the bonus cannot be achieved under either of the circumstances described in a) and c). Therefore some degree of co-operation is essential. The bogey of +120 was determined so that it would be possible to gain the bonus if agreement was obtained at the last negotiation, with certain reservations. The best possible explanation is a mathematical one, as follows:

Supposing we neglect, for the time being, the possibility of 6:5:4 being played. The cumulative net points which can be won are shown in column two of Table 2 below. Columns 3 and 4 show the points won in each round by agreement to play 1:2:3. Column 5 shows the possible total points which, at any stage in the game, could be won if the three syndicates chose to co-operate from that stage onwards. Adding the points already accrued from a win/lose situation (Col. 2) to the points remaining to be won (Col. 5) gives the maximum obtainable final score at each point (shown in Col. 6).

Examination of this column shows that even if win/lose points have been won, up to and including round 7, it is still possible to achieve the bonus, which could therefore form the basis of the final negotiations. It was on this basis, in fact, that the figure of 120 was chosen.

There is one other possibility which must be considered. If the 6:5:4 situation arises, this has a profound effect upon the attainment of the bonus, since a net score in any non-bonus round of −9 instead of +6 makes a difference of −15 to the total net score. By examination of Column 6 in the table, it can be deduced that if such an event takes place in the first three rounds, it is still possible, at the first negotiation, to legislate to win the bonus. (The net score after four rounds would be +15 instead of +30, and with 108 points available if co-operation commenced in round 5 would give a final total of 15 + 108 = 123). At round 7, however, it is no longer possible to negotiate to win the bonus, because the actual score after round 7 would be + 45 and the remaining points available through co-operation equal +63 (63 + 45 = 108). This explanation is clearly very complex mathematically; it is given here in full in order that tutors can have a degree of confidence in the mechanism of the exercise as a whole.

The bonus constraints can be summarised as follows:

1 The bonus can still be won at the last negotiated period, provided that a 6:5:4 situation has not arisen.
2 The bonus can be won at the first negotiation period provided that a 6:5:4 situation has arisen on not more than one occasion.
3 The bonus can only be won if the 1:2:3 situation arises on at least two occasions, one of which must be round 10.

	1	2	3	4	5	6
Round no.	Net points Win/lose	Cumulative points Win/lose	Net points Co-op.	Cum. points Co-op.	Total available	Total available if switch to Co-op.
1	+6	+6	+9	+9	+153	+153
2	+6	+12	+9	+18	+144	+150
3	+6	+18	+9	+27	+135	+147
4*	+12	+30	+18	+45	+126	+144
5	+6	+36	+9	+54	+108	+138
6	+6	+42	+9	+63	+99	+135
7*	+18	+60	+27	+90	+90	+132
8	+6	+66	+9	+99	+66	+123
9	+6	+72	+9	+108	+54	+120
10*	+30	+102	+45	+153	+45	+117

Table 2

Tutor's notes

These notes apply to the following four exercises:

Development Targets for *Jane Ryder; A Staff Development Programme for Jeremy Isis; Scenario 1; Scenario 2*.

Although intended mainly for in-service work with teachers, the exercise can be used successfully with older pupils and students.

The most appropriate use for all four exercises is to allow each group member some time to complete the task individually. Small groups (4 or 5 members each) are then formed and asked to produce a group solution which can then be displayed to the whole group. If possible, the small-group process could be observed, and observers asked to comment.

The total time for each of the exercises can be up to an hour.

DEVELOPMENT TARGETS FOR JANE RYDER

Jane is a Main Professional Grade teacher with a B Ed, degree newly married, aged 24, with one year's teaching experience. She passed her probationary year very successfully. She found teaching suited her admirably. Her discipline is sound, her relationships are good though staff find her a little conceited and irritating. All her work with her class of eight-year-olds is prepared and marked well. She teaches effectively, and it is clear from the comments of parents and from looking at children's work that she has real ability. Her administration is first class in all aspects of school life. She has one weakness with pupils which is a tendency to become too informal, and then to over-react if pupils are informal in return. During one incident she over-reacted and struck a boy on the head. She bitterly regretted the incident, though she still tends to flare up from time to time. A further weakness is her apparent inability to cope with some aspects of group work.

She is keen to gain promotion.

Jane wishes to accept responsibility for training, running and arranging fixtures for the netball team and taking them to matches. She has also offered to lead a school trip to Cornwall where she has recently been undertaking summer holiday work in a youth holiday camp. She is now approaching the mid-point of her second year of teaching.

If you were Jane Ryder's Head, what targets would you wish to set with her for the next 12 months?

A STAFF DEVELOPMENT PROGRAMME FOR JEREMY ISIS

Your are a member of staff with some responsibility for staff development at Loweswater Comprehensive School (Group 10, 11–18), serving a predominantly urban catchment area in a Northern LEA. The school has, for this LEA, an above average number of children with special needs.

The Head and Governors have recently appointed an Incentive Allowance B History Head of Department, Mr J R (Jeremy) Isis. He is well-qualified (MA Cantab) with references that were supportive without being ecstatic. The field was a thin one (Loweswater, on closer examination, belies its name), but Mr Isis impressed the Headteacher and Governors and, with the support of the LEA Adviser who was present at the interview, was appointed. Mr Isis had previously been an enthusiastic second person in a small history department in a well regarded, tightly-streamed comprehensive in central Berkshire.

Within a term of Mr Isis's arrival at Loweswater, it was becoming obvious to most staff, particularly senior and middle management, that he was facing difficulties in his work. He has problems with pupil control and seems to lack confidence in dealing with the other two staff of his own department. Relationships with heads of department and other senior staff appear to be slow to develop.

Devise a development programme for Mr Isis, covering the next 12 months.

© Bill Dennison, Roger Kirk   Blackwell   1990

SCENARIO 1

A teacher, Jane Smith, is a bright young woman with four years' teaching experience. Her husband holds a good position as a reporter with the local TV Channel. He is to take a six-week trip overseas during September and October to make a documentary for his station. Jane speaks to you during June to seek your cooperation in her appeal for leave without pay to accompany her husband.

Would you:
a) **Encourage Jane and say that you will strongly recommend that she be granted the leave?**
b) **Tell her that such requests make school management very difficult and could jeopardise work with her class as you may not easily get a suitable replacement, but you will help where you can?**
c) **Tell Jane that you will not recommend her leave?**
d) **Take some other action (please specify)?**

SCENARIO 2

A teacher, Geoff Scrivens, comes to see you about getting an extra day off before the holidays begin, because his wife has mistaken the dates for the holidays and has booked a flight a day before the end of term. At this time of year, four weeks before the end of term, it would be difficult to change to another flight, as Geoff has already discovered.

Would you:
a) **Grant his request?**
b) **Warn him that this is a serious matter but you will overlook it this time and cover for him?**
c) **Tell him that he will have to put in a form for leave without pay and face the consequences?**
d) **Take some other action (please specify)?**

GREAT EGGSPECTATIONS

Aim
- to enable group members to observe and test their assumptions about decision making, risk taking and understanding of process

Equipment

Two fresh eggs, two sheets of 40cm × 40cm paper, a roll of sellotape, two balloons, a piece of string approximately 200cm long and a pair of scissors.

Brief

Before the end of the allotted length of time for this project, a member of your group will go to the window and drop/throw an egg towards the ground. The egg should fall free and unattached and land intact and unbroken. During this descent, the egg may not come into contact with anything or anyone. You may not change the composition of the egg in any way, but you may use the materials provided (and ONLY those materials) to enhance the chances of success.

Your group has the option to make two attempts to achieve its objective but you may not use any of the materials (or any part of them) more than once.

Constraints
- Nobody is allowed within one metre cubed of the landing area of the egg.
- The window may only be opened to make an attempt.

Tutor's notes

The brief is unambiguous and over a period of time six ways of successfully completing the activity have been devised. In the main these have involved various catching devices, using the sellotape and the paper. Alternatively, the egg can be dropped straight on to the ground, provided the ground is reasonably soft (grass or soil) and the egg lands 'endways'. A first floor window is suitable, although higher levels have still produced 'successful' landings.

CENTIPEDE

Aims
- Problem-solving, coordination, communication

Materials
Each team of up to 10 people will need 2 long planks and 2 slings of about 60cm in length for each person (or one length of rope for the whole group instead of all the slings).

A course (suggested length 30m) needs to be marked out.

Brief
Using the 2 planks and the slings/ropes you are to transport yourself over a given stretch of ground, without any part of anyone's body touching the ground. Only one foot per person is allowed on each plank. If any part of anyone's body touches the ground the whole team must start again.

Tutor's notes
Completing the task is less significant than the processes it initiates, and the *Review* of them that follows. Nevertheless, for successful completion certain criteria must be observed:

a) The two planks must be kept parallel.
b) Everyone must face in the same direction.
c) Everyone must have a foot on each plank.
d) The ropes are used to lift the planks in a 'synchronised' way.

APPRAISAL ACTIVITY – 'I'll help you improve your driving'

Objectives

- to heighten awareness of the wider issues in appraisal
- to study some 'real' everyday behaviour and experience the feelings around personal competence and assessment of it
- to give feedback on the unconscious choices which we make when we engage in appraisal

The activity

The various components of this activity are:

1 Introduction (*5 minutes*)

2 Forming groups of three/trios (*5 minutes*)

3 Briefing (*5 minutes*)

4 The driving activity (*up to 40 minutes*)

5 The appraisal discussion (*30 minutes*)

6 Immediate expression of feeling (*5 minutes*)

7 Review of appraisal activity (*40 minutes*)

8 Discussion on wider issues arising (*30 minutes*)

Tutor's notes – some issues in appraisal
What is appraisal for?

- For reviewing past performance? For improving future performance? For comparing one person with another? For helping the organisation to be more effective? For helping the appraiser to be more effective? For evaluating different jobs?
- Should the person being appraised give comment and feedback to the appraiser?
- How important is observation?
- Should we call for evidence?
- Is appraisal concerned with the past or the future? If we examine the past we can do nothing about it. Perhaps we should only be interested in the future?
- People often see the past differently. Discussion could focus on: who should take the credit for a successful venture? Why did something less successful seem like a good idea at the time?

The appraisal interview/discussion

There are various ways of running this. It can be self-appraisal, where the appraisee does most of the analysis, prompted by helpful interventions from the other peron. Or, at the other extreme, appraisal can be about 'telling'. In this appraising style, we assume that the appraisers are accurate in their observations and it is simply lack of knowledge which prevents the appraisee improving. Or, we can have an interview of the 'tell-and-sell' type where suggestions are made for improvement and encouraging reasons are given for why it would be beneficial to do things rather differently. Or, we can have 'joint problem-solving' interviews where a more equal discussion is held on the basis of 'how things could be better' and 'who needs to do what'.

Most people new to appraisal or even those who have operated appraisal 'systems' are not conscious of the variety of options. It is helpful for people to be aware of the variety of choices – because what they do in terms of observation and discussion will be very different depending on which objectives they take.

Activity
The exercise is a 20–30 minute sample of driving several miles around a varied course. The route need not be specified exactly but should be long enough to include a variety of hazards (eg emerging from a side road, going at some speed along an urban street or country lane and passing through some occupied areas where issues of safety and, perhaps, consideration for others will arise).

In some ways this is a two-level session, because after the drive the appraisers become the centre of attention in terms of how they handled the appraising situation rather than continuing to focus on the drivers and their driving.

Driving is chosen because it is a common activity, which most of us feel we do (at least) quite well although there are wide variations in how people judge it (eg safety, speed, risk-taking under conditions when you cannot see what the dangers might be, comfort of passengers, consideration for the car itself, etc). Some of these considerations are important for most of us but others are hardly thought about at all by some people. This means that the appraiser can be looking at some aspects of performance which hardly enter the head of the driver and vice-versa.

Forming trios
After sorting out practical questions (who can drive, who has a car etc) groups of three should be formed where one person is the driver (appraisee), another is appraiser and the third, sitting in the back, is the observer of the whole process. If after forming trios you have one or two people left over, you can have two observers in a group.

Briefing
Outline the stages of the exercise privately to the observers. They do not take part in the driving or appraisal at all. Their job is to observe and make notes. They are concerned with the behaviour of the appraiser. They do not need to spend energy making their own assessment of driving.

The driving activity
Do not in any way push the trio to get started. Having given them the task and time limits let them start in their own time – to see if they *do* prepare before the activity. Most people should but do not.

The appraisal discussion
'We now have 30 minutes within which you should do whatever preparation is necessary and then conduct, or at least begin, the appraisal discussion'.

It can be useful to tape record this discussion. The observer is encouraged to continue to be the silent 'fly on the wall', and should not contribute personal views of the driving.

The immediate expression of feelings

After the appraisal discussion the trio participants should be asked to consider their feelings about the interview.

First, as a demonstration of good practice, to the appraiser 'How do you feel, in a few words, the interview/discussion went?'

Secondly, to the appraisee 'How do you feel, in a few words, about the discussion you've just taken part in about your driving?'

Review of appraisal activity

Observers should give feedback to appraisers, descriptively rather than evaluatively, on what they noticed which seemed to be helpful, what seemed not to be helpful, and what it might have been useful to do, commenting on what (seemed to be) the reactions of the appraisee (the driver).

The results can then be brought together: 'What are some of the things we've learned about appraisal from the exercise?' etc.

Planning review

Assemble the different main learning points, using questions (after each group has contributed) such as 'How many appraisers took time to gather their thoughts before starting the interview? Why might that have been helpful?' etc.

Some typical outcomes

Appraisers rarely discuss with the appraisee the basis of the forthcoming appraisal. They frequently do not list (for themselves) the factors or criteria upon which they will do the appraisal. They hardly ever ask the appraisee (the driver) what aspects of their performance they would like observed and given feedback on. They frequently start the exercise and begin the observation without preparation. They often do not recognise that situations which are experienced together can be seen quite differently by other people. They frequently do not take time (after the observation) to gather their thoughts, review their observations, and *prepare* for the appraisal discussion. They rarely take the opportunity to invite the appraisee to review the performance privately before the discussion. Some (but not many) appraisers begin the appraisal discussion by asking appraisees for their initial feelings and reactions.

All these options are available (to be taken or ignored) given that the tutor does not put too much pressure of time on structuring the activity and makes a point of saying clearly (but without over-emphasising) 'When you are ready and in your own time, please start the activity'.

This activity has been used several times with groups of managers and of teachers and usually generates interest and appreciation of the wider aspects of appraisals. The driving was 'real' and the feelings generated perhaps less intense (than about one's job performance) but still genuine.